The
Sandlapper
Cookbook

The Sandlapper Cookbook

compiled by
Catha W. Reid
and
Joseph T. Bruce, Jr.

First Edition
Second Printing

The Sandlapper Store, Inc., Lexington, S.C.

FIRST EDITION
Second Printing

ISBN # 0-87844-020-8

The Sandlapper Store, Inc.
P.O. Box 841
Lexington, S.C. 29072

To the loyal readers of Sandlapper magazine

Contents

Photographs

Preface

The South has long been recognized for the high quality of its cuisine. As a Southern magazine, *Sandlapper* has, since its beginning, reflected this culinary tradition by frequently publishing recipes from some of South Carolina's best cooks. *Sandlapper's* loyal readers have continued to respond quite favorably to this particular feature of the magazine and have often sent their own favorite recipes. It was this enthusiasm on the part of our readers which first suggested the idea of *The Sandlapper Cookbook*. Through notices in the magazine and personal letters to our readers, we have expanded our stock of recipes to its present size. From South Carolina as well as from places outside our state's boundaries, recipes accumulated. We offer them now to you with the hope that they will provide many hours of cooking and eating pleasure.

We wish especially to express our appreciation to Agnes Nelson, whose skill as a typesetter and dedication to our task have been invaluable. And of course our special thanks go to each person who kindly submitted recipes.

CWR
JTB, Jr.

August 22, 1973
Columbia, South Carolina

Appetizers

CHEESE WAFERS

½ cup fat (1 stick margarine)
2 cups grated sharp cheese
  (½ lb.)
1 cup plain flour

1/8 tsp. red pepper
½ tsp. salt
½ cup chopped pecans

Cream fat; add grated cheese, sifted dry ingredients and nuts. Form in rolls, wrap in wax paper, and chill. When firm, slice and bake on cookie sheet at 375⁰ for about 12 minutes. Set wafers to cool on a flour sack or brown paper.

Miss Martha Hearon
Bishopville

CHEESE BALLS

1 stick oleo, room temperature
  (not melted)
1 cup finely grated sharp cheese

1 cup plain flour
1 cup Rice Krispies

Mix thoroughly oleo, cheese and flour. Add Rice Krispies last. Pinch off very small pieces of dough and shape into small balls. Place on cookie sheet and bake slowly until brown.

Miss Clara L. Hughes
Woodruff

CHEESE DAISIES

¾ cup butter
1½ cup sharp cheddar cheese
  (grated)
¼ cup Parmesan cheese
  (grated)

1½ cups flour
¾ tsp. paprika
1 tsp. salt

Cream butter with cheese. Sift together flour, paprika, and salt. Add this to the creamed mixture and stir well. Press through cookie press onto baking sheet. Bake at 350⁰. Makes about 24 daisies.

Mrs. Frederick (Jane) Haynes, Jr.
Spartanburg

3

CHEESE WAFERS

1 lb. margarine (cream well)
1 lb. medium sharp cheddar
  cheese (grated fine)
4½ cups plain flour (sifted before
  measuring)

1 tsp. salt
Red pepper (sprinkle
  sparingly over flour)

Cream margarine, add grated cheese and mix together well. Add flour and salt. When blended together shape dough on large dinner plate, cover and chill overnight. Remove from refrigerator few minutes, roll out to desired thickness, cut wafers with 1½ inch round cutter. Place on ungreased cookie sheet, cook 350⁰ over 10 to 12 minutes. Makes 150 wafers.

Mrs. L. Marion Gressette
St. Matthews

CHEESE FLUFFS

2 sticks butter
½ lb. sharp cheese
2 cups flour

¼ tsp. salt
1/8 tsp. red pepper
2 cups Rice Krispies

Mix well. Drop by teaspoon onto cookie sheet. Bake at 375⁰.

Mrs. Willard Davis
Columbia

CHEESE ROLL

1 lb. grated cheese
1 small pkg. softened
  cream cheese

Salt or onion salt
Worcestershire sauce

Mix grated cheese with cream cheese. Season with salt or onion salt and Worcestershire sauce. Form into a roll, and roll in paprika, coating outside. Chill before slicing.

Mrs. J. W. Waddill
Columbia

CREAM CHEESE ROLL

2 (8 oz.) pkgs. cream cheese (softened)
1 (8½ oz.) can crushed pineapple (drained)

2 cups finely chopped pecans
¼ cup finely chopped green pepper
2 Tbs. finely chopped onion
1 Tbs. seasoned salt (optional)

Mix cream cheese, pineapple, pepper, onion, salt and ½ of the nuts. Form into a log or ball and roll in other half of the nuts. Refrigerate overnight. Serve with unsalted crackers. Serves 25 or 30.

Mrs. Frances Peebles Byars
Easley

CREAM CHEESE DIP

2 (3 oz.) pkgs. cream cheese
½ cup French dressing (see below)
1 tsp. cream style horseradish

Few drops Worcestershire sauce
1 tsp. chopped parsley
Garlic (optional)
1 egg

Mash cheese. Blend in French dressing and add other ingredients.

French Dressing

2 tsp. salt
1 tsp. sugar
½ tsp. pepper

1½ cups salad oil
1 tsp. paprika
½ cup lemon juice

Combine and shake well in a covered jar.

Mrs. Allen B. Thomas
Aiken

5

CHILI-CHEESE DIP

1 can chili (without beans)
1 (8 oz.) jar Cheez-whiz
1 can French-fried onion rings

Combine and heat in a small saucepan over medium heat until smooth. Serve hot with Fritos. May be frozen and reheated.

Earle Traynham
Columbia

CURRY DIP

1 cup mayonnaise
3 Tbs. catsup
3 tsp. curry powder

1 tsp. lemon juice
1 clove garlic (minced)
1 Tbs. Worcestershire sauce

Mix all ingredients and let stand in refrigerator 24 hours. (Double for a crowd.) Use fresh vegetables to dip—broccoli, cauliflower, carrots, or celery. Serve cold.

Mary Anne Crocker
Alexandria, Virginia

HOT CHEESE OLIVES

¼ lb. margarine
1 (8 oz.) pkg. grated cracker
  barrel cheese
1 cup flour

1 tsp. paprika
½ tsp. salt
1½ bottles small stuffed
  olives

Knead ingredients into dough. Roll 1 teaspoon of dough around a dry olive. Bake at 425^0 for 10 to 15 minutes. Makes approximately 60 balls. This recipe may be made ahead of time and frozen.

Mrs. T. Dewey Wise
Mt. Pleasant

WEINER FONDU

1 pkg. weiners (cut in small
    pieces)
1 jar currant jelly

1 small jar prepared mustard
Dash Tabasco and
    Worcestershire sauce

Melt mustard and jelly over medium heat. Add weiners and bring to boil. Simmer for 1 hour. Transfer to fondu pot. Serve as hot hors d'oeuvres.

Mrs. Earle C. Traynham, Jr.
Columbia

WEST INDIAN BANANAS IN WINE

6 bananas
2 Tbs. flour
1 cup dry white wine

Dash nutmeg, cinnamon,
    and cloves
1 Tbs. butter

Peel and halve bananas. Put in saucepan. Add wine and a dash of salt. Cover. Bring to a boil, and then simmer gently for about 25 minutes. Blend butter, flour, and spices. Add gradually, stirring to banana mixture. Serve as a vegetable with duck or chicken.

Mr. and Mrs. R. D. Coble
Pensacola, Florida

PARTY MIX

1/3 cup salad oil
1 Tbs. Worcestershire sauce
1 tsp. salt
1/8 tsp. garlic salt or powder

2 cups shredded wheat, bite size
2 cups shredded rice, bite size
1½ cups pretzel sticks
½ cup pecans

Heat oven to 300°. Measure oil into cup. Add Worcestershire sauce, salt and garlic salt and beat with fork. Put cereals and nuts into a shallow baking pan. Pour oil mixture over cereal mixture. Stir to coat all pieces. Bake 30 minutes, stirring every 10 minutes. Spread on paper towels to cool. Makes 6 cups.

Mrs. Allen B. Thomas
Aiken

Beverages

BAPTIST PUNCH

10 cups sugar
5 Tbs. citric acid
(can be purchased at drug store)
2 large cans pineapple juice

14 cups water
8 tsp. vanilla flavoring
8 tsp. almond flavoring

Mix together until dissolved and then add 9 quarts of water. Freeze 1/3 of punch for ice and remove from freezer several hours before use. When serving add 4 bottles of ginger ale (quart size) or more, to taste. Add the food coloring you desire for color.

Mrs. W. Frank Partridge, Jr.
Newberry

PUNCH

2 oz. citric acid
(powder form)
1 large can orange juice
(frozen 12 oz.)

1 large can pineapple juice
(frozen 12 oz.)
2 gal. water
6 cups sugar

Mix all ingredients together. Chill and serve. Makes 9-10 quarts. Serves approximately 100.

Mrs. J. L. Martin
West Columbia

CITRIC ACID PUNCH

2 oz. citric acid crystals
2 qts. boiling water
1 tall can pineapple juice

1 can concentrated orange
juice
5 qts. cold water
6 cups sugar

Add citric acid crystals to boiling water, let soak 24 hours (not in metal container). Add pineapple juice, orange juice, and cold water. Stir in sugar. Serves 50.

Mrs. Thyra S. Robinson
Lake Placid, Florida

GOLDEN PUNCH

1 (46 oz.) can orange juice
1 (46 oz.) can pineapple juice
1 large frozen orange juice,
  diluted as directed
1 large frozen lemonade, diluted
  as directed

1 qt. strong black tea
1 qt. gingerale
1 qt. orange sherbet

Mix orange juice, pineapple juice and lemonade. Stir well and add black tea. When ready to serve, add gingerale and orange sherbet.

Mrs. Odd Thorsen
Rock Hill

GOOD CLEAR GREEN PUNCH

1 pkg. lemon-lime
2 cups hot water
1½ cups sugar
5 cups cold water

Juice 3 lemons
1 large can pineapple juice
1 large bottle ginger ale
  (added at serving time)

Mix all ingredients well. Add ginger ale before serving. Serves 20-25.

Mrs. Charles E. Calhoun
Clio

BEST YEAR ROUND PUNCH

4 (28 oz.) bottles of ginger ale
½ gal. orange (or your favorite) sherbet

Place sherbet in punch bowl and pour the 4 bottles of gingerale over it—you can begin serving immediately as the sherbet melts. You have 112 ozs. of gingerale and 64 ozs. of sherbet—total of 176 ozs. Divide the size of your cups into this and you'll know exactly how many servings you have.

Mrs. Benny B. Berry
St. George

COFFEE DIABLO

2 cups brandy
2 cups strong French coffee
Spiral peel 1 orange

1 doz. cloves
1 stick cinnamon
2 cubes sugar

Put all except the coffee into a metal tureen. Light and stir gently with large ladle. After 1 minute, slowly pour in the coffee. Serve in demitasses.

Mrs. Doris Herring
Columbia

COFFEE DELIGHT

½ lb. marshmallows
1 cup strong coffee

½ pint whipped cream
1 doz. lady fingers

Melt marshmallows in coffee. Cool and fold in whipped cream. Pour mixture in bowl and place lady fingers around it. Serves 8.

Mrs. Van Noy Thornhill
Charleston

INSTANT SPICED TEA

18 oz. jar Tang
2 oz. jar plain instant Nestea
½ pkg. (3 oz.) Twist lemonade mix

½ tsp. ground cinnamon
½ tsp. ground cloves

Mix all ingredients together thoroughly and store in glass jar or pitcher. When ready for use, add 2 teaspoons to each cup of boiling water. Add sugar to sweeten.

Mrs. Winfield K. Sharp, III
Anderson

INSTANT RUSSIAN TEA

1 cup Tang
1 cup sugar
½ cup instant lemon flavored
  tea (not pre-sweetened)

1 tsp. powdered cloves
1 tsp. powdered cinnamon

Mix well and use two heaping teaspoons with each cup of hot water.

Mrs. Rose Wilkins
Lexington

Breads

THE SOUTH CAROLINA HUSH PUPPY

There are countless stories explaining the origins of this traditional South Carolina treat. Most conjure up a picture of lazy hound dogs slinking under the dusty porches of rural shacks Tobacco Road style, their yapping quieted only by tossing them these tasty morsels of fried bread. Others visualize a more aristocratic scene: scarlet-liveried fox hunters hushing their excited hounds after the hunt with small bits of corn bread.

This particular recipe was served by a Girl Scout troop from South Carolina at a national round-up in Idaho. Girls from all over the country requested the recipe and took it home to serve.

1 cup water ground corn meal
¼ cup flour
2 tsp. baking powder
½ cup milk
1 finely chopped onion
½ tsp. salt
1 egg

Mix corn meal, flour, baking powder and salt. Break in egg and start beating. Slowly add milk. Beat like the Evil One until mixture becomes a paste. Drop a gob from a spoon into deep, hot grease. Remove when golden brown.

Helen Ann Rawlinson
West Columbia

HUSH PUPPIES

¾ cup plain flour
¾ cup corn meal
Salt to taste
½ stick butter or margarine, or equivalent fat from fried fish
(optional)
1 heaping Tbs. baking powder
1½ cups onions (finely chopped)
2 eggs (slightly beaten)

Liquid thinner: buttermilk, sweet milk, beer, or tomato juice
(optional)

Mix dry ingredients thoroughly, stir in eggs (and melted butter or fat if desired). Add selected liquid thinner until entire batter is brought to an "easy drop" consistency. Use a tablespoon to drop blobs of batter about the size of hickory nuts into hot fat (375^0) and cook to a golden brown (3 to 5 minutes).

Mr. Robert L. Walker
Orlando, Florida

13

SANDLAPPER AWENDAW CORN BREAD

1 cup boiled big-grain hominy
2 egg yolks (lightly beaten)
½ tsp. butter or margarine
1 cup milk

1 cup cornmeal
¾ tsp. salt
2 egg whites (stiffly beaten)

Stir hominy into egg yolks; add butter or margarine, then milk. Gradually stir in cornmeal and salt; fold in stiffly beaten egg whites. Batter should resemble a custard at this point. Pour into a buttered 1½ quart baking pan and bake at 325⁰ for 45 minutes to 1 hour. Yield: 4 servings.

Mrs. John Drummond
Ninety Six

CORN BREAD

1 cup corn meal (sifted)
1 cup buttermilk
1 egg
½ tsp. baking powder

½ tsp. baking soda
½ tsp. salt
4 Tbs. bacon drippings (or
    melted shortening)

Mix dry ingredients in bowl. Add buttermilk mixed with egg. Add 2 tablespoons of shortening last. Heat remaining 2 tablespoons in iron pan and pour batter into the pan. Batter should sear when hitting the pan. Bake in 450⁰ oven until dark brown on top. Corn bread will be crisp on bottom. Turn out bread on a plate and slice.

Harry D. Smith
Atlanta, Georgia

MEXICAN CORN BREAD

1 cup cream style corn
½ cup milk
1/3 cup oil
2 eggs (slightly beaten)
1½ cups grated sharp N.Y.
    State cheese

½ tsp. soda
1 cup corn meal (self-rising)
1 small can chili peppers
    (red or green, rinsed and
    cut up)

Mix all ingredients except cheese and peppers. Pour half of batter into large greased baking dish, spread with peppers, then cheese, then pour remaining batter on top. Bake at 400⁰ for 30 minutes or so. Serve in squares or small wedges while hot.

Lydia C. Burriss
Greenville

SALLY LUNN

4 Tbs. shortening
4 Tbs. sugar
1 tsp. salt
2 cups sifted flour (plain)

4 tsp. baking powder
1 egg
¾ cup milk (a whole cup may be used if desired)

Cream shortening, sugar, and salt together. Sift flour and baking powder together. Add well-beaten egg to creamed mixture. Add flour and milk alternately, making a smooth batter. Bake in a greased pan in moderately hot oven (425⁰) for 25 minutes.

Miss Martha Frances Morgan
Greenville

SALLY LUNN BREAD

¾ cup milk
2 Tbs. sugar
1 tsp. salt
2 Tbs. shortening
1 pkg. yeast

¼ cup warm (not hot) water
2¾ cups flour
1 egg

Scald milk. Add sugar, salt, shortening. Stir to dissolve. Pour into mixing bowl. Cool to lukewarm. While milk cools, sprinkle dry yeast into warm water. Stir until dissolved. To cooled milk, add 2 cups flour. Mix well, then beat until smooth. Stir in dissolved yeast. Add egg and beat at least 1 minute. Stir in remaining flour and beat until smooth (about 2 minutes). Scrape batter down from side of bowl. Cover and let rise 1 hour. Stir down and turn batter into greased loaf pan and let rise 1 hour. Bake at 350⁰ for 45 minutes.

Mrs. J. W. Waddill
Columbia

GRANDMA'S SWEDISH BREAD

My grandmother was a wonderful cook of the "Old Country" school. She was Swedish and spent all day in the kitchen cooking without recipes and without measuring cups! Her most famous treat was her homemade bread.

1 qt. lukewarm water	12 cups flour
(or potato water)	1 tsp. salt (heaping)
1 yeast cake	1 cup graham flour

Remove 1 cup water and dissolve yeast cake in it. Add 6 cups flour to remaining water. Mix. Add dissolved yeast. Let rise in a warm place. Add 1 teaspoon salt and 1 cup graham flour. Mix. Add 6 cups flour. Knead well. Flour board, knead again. Grease top of batter and let rise double. Shape loaves on floured board and let rise double. Bake at 375^0 until golden brown, about 30 minutes. Butter top of loaves while still warm.

Mrs. Strom Thurmond
Aiken

WHOLE WHEAT HONEY LOAVES

3 cups water	Optional:
¾ cup honey	1 cup oatmeal
3 pkgs. yeast	1 cup raisins
8 cups whole wheat flour	1 cup chopped nuts
2 tsp. salt	

Warm water and honey. Add yeast and let grow 5 to 10 minutes. Add 5 cups flour and salt. Beat on slow speed 7 minutes. Then beating or stirring with spoon slowly add 2 to 3 cups flour (or 1 to 2 cups flour and oatmeal, raisins, and nuts). Turn out on floured bread board and let rest 5 minutes. Knead smooth. Place in greased bowl. Cover with cloth and let rise until double. (For a more moist loaf, place bowl on rack in oven over pot of boiling hot water and close oven door, replace water as it cools). Knead and form into 3 loaves and put into greased loaf pans. For tender crust, grease top of loaves. Let double. Bake at 325^0 for 45 minutes. Turn off oven and let remain in oven 10 more minutes. (To test: tap bottom of loaf and if sounds hollow, the loaf is done). Let cool on sides on wire rack.

Jack Belk
Orangeburg

HERB BREAD

2 pkg. dry yeast
1 cup milk
¼ cup sugar
¼ cup shortening
2 tsp. salt
5 cups sifted flour

2 eggs
¼ tsp. dried basil
¼ tsp. dried thyme
¼ tsp. dried oregano
½ tsp. nutmeg

Soften yeast in ¼ cup warm water and set aside. Scald milk. Mix sugar, shortening and salt, then add milk, and cool to lukewarm. Add 2 cups sifted flour to make a thick batter and mix well. Stir in softened yeast and eggs. Crumble basil, thyme, and oregano and add to batter along with nutmeg. Beat well. Add 2½ to 3 cups (even more if necessary) until a soft dough is formed. Turn out on a lightly floured board or pastry cloth. Knead about 5 minutes or until dough is smooth and satiny. Place in a greased bowl, cover, and let rise until doubled in bulk (1½ to 2 hours). When light, punch down. Divide dough into 2 equal parts and shape into a smooth ball. Let rest for 10 minutes. Shape into loaves and place in well-greased pans. Let rise for 1 hour and bake 35 minutes at 375⁰.

Miss Lucile Huggin
Rock Hill

APPLE BREAD

This recipe took top honors in a bake-off at the 1971 Apple Festival in Westminister.

½ cup shortening
1 cup sugar
1 egg
2 cups flour
2 cups peeled chopped apples

2/3 cup nuts
1 tsp. baking soda
½ tsp. ground cloves
1 tsp. cinnamon
1 tsp. salt

Cream shortening with sugar. Add egg, mix well. Stir in dry ingredients. Add apples and nuts. Mixture is thick and may require ¼ cup water. Put in greased and floured loaf pan and bake for 1 hour at 350⁰. Dust with confectioners' sugar.

Mrs. William C. Mann
Seneca

BANANA BREAD

2 cups sifted flour
1 tsp. baking soda
1 tsp. salt
1 tsp. vanilla
1 stick margarine

1 cup sugar
2 eggs
1 cup mashed rip bananas
¼ cup sour cream
1 cup chopped pecans or walnuts

Sift flour, baking soda and salt. Cream margarine and sugar; add vanilla and beat thoroughly. Eggs should be added one at a time, beating thoroughly each time. Blend in bananas, do not beat hard. Add dry ingredients, one-third at a time, alternating with sour cream in halves. Pour batter into two baking pans (3½ x 7 inches) with greased oil paper in bottom. Bake about 45 minutes at 350⁰ —or until bread tests done. Cool on wire racks.

Alice Watson
Clemson

BANANA BREAD

½ cup butter
2 eggs
1½ cups sugar
2 cups plain flour

1 tsp. vanilla
1 tsp. soda
½ cup buttermilk
3 bananas (mashed)

Cream butter and sugar. Sift flour and soda together; add eggs. Add flour alternately with buttermilk. Add vanilla and bananas. Bake in tube pan at 325⁰ for about an hour. Test with straw to determine if done.

Mrs. J. L. Martin
West Columbia

ORANGE BREAD

Peels of 4 oranges
½ tsp. baking soda
2½ cups sugar
2 eggs (beaten)
½ cup milk

2½ cups flour
3 tsp. baking powder
½ tsp. salt
½ cup pecans or walnuts
2 Tbs. melted butter or margarine

Cut orange peels into thin slivers, cover with water, add ½ teaspoon soda and bring to a boil. Simmer 15 minutes and drain,

18

then rinse with cold water. Barely cover peel again with fresh water, add 2 cups sugar and cook over low heat until peel is candied (223⁰ on candy thermometer) about 1-1½ hours. Set aside in colander to drain and cool. When ready to make bread, combine in a large bowl 2 beaten eggs, ½ cup milk, ½ cup sugar. Stir in 2½ cups flour that has been sifted with 3 teaspoons baking powder and ½ teaspoon salt. Mix in nuts, candied peel, and melted butter. Place in buttered loaf pan and bake at 350⁰ for 1 hour.

Mrs. Rufus D. Elliott
Chattanooga, Tennessee

MOLASSES BRAN BREAD

1 cup bran (ready to eat)	¾ cup hot water
½ cup seedless raisins	1 egg
2 Tbs. shortening	1 cup flour
½ cup molasses	1 tsp. baking soda
½ tsp. salt	1 tsp. cinnamon

Measure bran, raisins, shortening and molasses into a mixing bowl. Add hot water and stir until shortening melts. Add egg and beat well. Sift together flour, salt, soda, and cinnamon. Add to bran mixture. Stir only until combined. Spread in a greased loaf pan (9½ x 4½ inches). Bake at 350⁰ about 35 minutes. Remove immediately from pan. Slice and serve hot—or serve cold with cream cheese—or toasted with butter.

Mrs. L. D. Coulter
Charleston

MY MUDD'S SPOON BREAD

1 cup corn meal	1 Tbs. baking powder
1 1/3 cups boiling water	4 Tbs. butter or margarine
1 1/3 cups fresh milk	1 1/3 tsp. sugar
3 whole eggs	1½ tsp. salt

Mix sugar and salt with corn meal and blend well. Pour boiling water over meal, stirring constantly. Let stand until cool. Beat eggs until light, add eggs and baking powder to mixture. Add milk and pour mixture into a 2-quart buttered pan or baking dish. Place in shallow pan of hot water in 350⁰ oven. Bake about 35 minutes. Serves 8.

Perribeth Scarborough
Hartsville

CHEESE GARLIC BREAD

1 long loaf Italian style or
  French style bread
2 sticks oleo (1 for each half)
Garlic powder or several cloves

2 cups grated cheese (cheddar,
  mild or sharp—to taste)
Oregano

Cut bread down the middle, making 2 parts. Melt oleo and add garlic. Spread over bread. Spread the grated cheese over loaves. Sprinkle with oregano. Bake at 425⁰ until bubbly brown. Cut with electric knife into wedges.

Mrs. Marvin H. Little
Ballentine

RIZ BISCUITS

1 cup buttermilk
1 pkg. yeast
1/3 cup Crisco
2½ cups self-rising flour

1 tsp. salt
¼ tsp. soda
1 Tbs. sugar

Warm milk, add yeast and mix well. Then mix with the other ingredients. Put in a warm place and let rise for 1 hour. Work down and cut biscuits. Brush top with melted butter; put another biscuit on top and press together. Let rise for 1 hour. Bake at 425⁰.

Mrs. Belle Scott
Clinton

"RIZ" BISCUITS

1 pkg. dry yeast
¼ cup lukewarm water
2½ cups sifted self-rising
  flour

1 Tbs. sugar
3 Tbs. shortening
½ cup buttermilk

Sprinkle the yeast in lukewarm water. Do not stir. Let stand 10 minutes. Sift together flour and sugar. Add the shortening and buttermilk to make a very light dough. Knead lightly. Roll out ¼ inch thick. Cut with biscuit cutter. Place half the biscuits on greased cookie sheet. Brush with melted butter. Place remaining rounds on top. Brush top with melted butter. Let biscuits rise for 45 to 60 minutes. Bake at 400⁰ for 10 to 12 minutes.

Mrs. Joe Long
Abbeville

SWEET POTATO BISCUITS

¾ cup mashed sweet potatoes
2/3 cup milk
4 Tbs. melted butter
1¼ cups flour, plain

4 tsp. baking powder
1 Tbs. sugar
½ tsp. salt

Mix mashed sweet potatoes, milk, and melted butter together. Add remaining ingredients, sifted all together, to make a soft dough. Turn out on floured board, and toss lightly until outside looks smooth. Roll out ½ inch thick, cut with floured biscuit cutter. Bake on greased pan in hot oven (450⁰) for about 15 minutes. Biscuits are excellent buttered when hot.

Miss Vera Edwards
Chester

BESSIE'S SWEET POTATO BISCUITS

1¼ cups sifted all-purpose flour
1 Tbs. baking powder
1 tsp. sugar
½ tsp. salt

3 Tbs. shortening
1 cup mashed sweet potato
½ cup milk

Sift flour, baking powder and salt. Add shortening, sweet potato and milk. Knead gently, and with hands pat biscuit ½ inch thick. Bake until brown.

Mrs. W. C. Horton
Beaufort

21

POTATO ROLLS

1 cup potatoes (mashed)	1 scant cup flour
2 Tbs. butter	½ yeast cake
2 cups lukewarm milk	1 tsp. salt
1 Tbs. sugar	

Dissolve yeast in warm water. Mix ingredients together using only ½ cup flour and leave mixture to rise overnight. Early the next morning, mix other ½ cup flour and knead thoroughly. Let rise for 1½ hours. After a second brisk hard kneading, mold into small rolls, set in pan, and leave in a warm place for ½ hour before baking. Serve hot.

Ann M. Aycock
Jonesville

SUNDAY ROLLS

½ cup warm water	1 yeast cake
½ cup sugar	7 cups flour
½ cup shortening	1 Tbs. salt

Dissolve yeast in warm water. Mix in separate bowl the sugar, shortening and salt. Add yeast to this mixture. Blend in flour (about 7 cups). After mixing well, place in refrigerator in bowl, covered with cloth, overnight. Next morning, make out rolls and and let stand several hours to rise before baking.

Mrs. E. L. Bolick
Central

ALABAMA MOUNTAIN MUFFINS

4 Tbs. shortening	½ tsp. salt
½ cup sugar	2/3 cup milk
3 eggs	2½ cups flour
3 tsp. baking powder	

Cream shortening and sugar together until very light, adding the yolks one at a time. Sift the flour, baking powder and salt. Add this alternately with the milk to the first mixture. Beat until smooth, then fold in the whites of eggs which have been beaten until stiff. Bake in well-greased muffin pan.

Mrs. Doris Herring
Columbia

SURPRISE MUFFINS

½ lb. dried fruit
2 eggs (well beaten)
1 cup sugar
½ cup lard or butter

1 cup milk
2 tsp. baking powder
1 tsp. vanilla
2 cups flour

Cook dried fruit, and when done, sweeten to taste. Cream sugar and lard or butter. Mix well beaten eggs with milk, baking powder, vanilla and flour. Grease muffin pans then add a spoonful of fruit, then a spoonful of dough alternately until muffin tin is ½ to 2/3 full. Bake in a moderate oven. Makes 18 muffins.

Mrs. Doris Herring
Columbia

MOTHER'S POP-OVERS

During my youth, in the early 1900s, toast was considered an abomination. Hot breads, biscuits, muffins, waffles, and hot cakes were generally served for breakfast and supper in well-ordered South Carolina homes. Pop-overs were an especial winter supper favorite, though just as welcome on a hot summer's evening if the cook was up to the heat of the kitchen.

1½ cups flour
½ tsp. salt
1½ cups milk

2 whole eggs
2 tsp. melted butter or margarine

Put flour and salt in bowl. Add milk and eggs. Beat with rotary beater 3 minutes. Add melted butter and stir. Put in well-greased muffin pans. Bake in hot oven 350⁰ for 40 minutes, makes 12 muffins. Serve piping hot with butter, preferably for supper or breakfast. Pop-overs should rise with thin crust at top, hollow inside and crust at bottoms.

Charles E. Thomas
Greenville

23

SUPER DUPER DROP DUMPLINGS

1 cup flour
2 tsp. baking powder
½ tsp. salt

1 egg
½ cup milk

Blend dry ingredients, then slowly add beaten egg and milk mixture until smoothly blended. Drop by tablespoonfuls into boiling stock; reduce heat so that liquid simmers and cook uncovered for 5 minutes, then cover and cook 10 to 15 minutes until cooked light and puffy.

Mr. & Mrs. R. D. Coble
Pensacola, Florida

AUNT SALLIE'S SWEET POTATO PONE

1 lb. sweet potatoes, grated
1 cup brown sugar
1 stick melted butter
1 tsp. salt

1 tsp. ginger
1 tsp. nutmeg
1 cup water

Mix well, bake one hour at 325⁰ in buttered baking dish.

Mrs. W. C. Horton
Beaufort

MY FAVORITE BUTTERMILK PANCAKES

1¼ cups self-rising flour
1 Tbs. sugar
1½ cups buttermilk

2 Tbs. liquid shortening
1 egg

Blend buttermilk, shortening, and egg in shaker; add liquid to flour and sugar. Stir with large spoon to obtain smooth consistency. Do not worry about flour lumps. Additional buttermilk may be necessary to achieve a smooth flowing mixture. Heat griddle to 400⁰ and maintain this heat. Pour batter from ¼ cup measuring device to form desired size. Cook on one side until bubbling ceases, usually when a shiny film appears on the pancake. Turn once and cook other side which will usually take a short time—result, the lightest and fluffiest pancakes you've ever eaten.

Mr. Henry O. Kemp
Newport News, Virginia

Desserts

Candy

BUTTERSCOTCH CANDY

3 pkg. butterscotch morsels
1 can Planters salted peanuts

1 can Chow Mein noodles

Melt morsels in double boiler. Add peanuts and noodles. Drop by spoonful on wax paper. Cool thoroughly (about 30 minutes).

Mrs. J. L. Martin
West Columbia

CHOCOLATE FUDGE

2 cups sugar
2 tsp. white Karo syrup
1 cup evaporated milk
4 Tbs. cocoa

1 tsp. vanilla
1 Tbs. butter
1 cup chopped nuts

Mix sugar, syrup, and milk in a saucepan and bring to boil. Add cocoa which has been diluted with water making a thin paste. Let boil (stirring often) until it forms a soft ball in water. Remove from stove. Let stand for 15 minutes. Add vanilla, butter, and nuts and beat until creamy. Pour out into buttered platter to cool. Cut in squares just before it gets hard.

Mrs. J. B. Traywick, II
Spartanburg

FOOLPROOF CHOCOLATE FUDGE

¼ lb. margarine
1 pkg. chocolate chips
1 cup nuts

1 small can evaporated milk
2 cups granulated sugar
12 marshmallows

Put margarine, chocolate chips, and nuts in mixing bowl. Boil together for six minutes the milk, sugar, and marshmallows. Then pour over the mixture in mixing bowl and stir until oleo and chocolate are melted. Pour on platter to cool. Cut in 1 inch squares.

Mrs. Henry O. Kemp
Newport News, Virginia

CHOCOLATE FUDGE

2 cups granulated sugar
1 cup light cream
2 squares unsweetened chocolate

1 cup 4X confectioners'
sugar
2 Tbs. butter
1 tsp. vanilla

Mix together in a heavy saucepan granulated sugar, light cream, chocolate, and confectioners' sugar. Heat until mixture forms a soft ball in cold water. Stir just enough to prevent sticking. Add butter and vanilla. Do not stir until lukewarm (110⁰). Beat by hand until stiff enough to be spread in an 8-inch buttered pan (or until it begins to lose its shine.)

Mrs. F. K. (Katherine) Simons, Jr.
Eutawville

Cakes

APPLE CAKE

1 cup butter or margarine
2 cups sugar
2 cups raisins
2 tsp. nutmeg
2 tsp. soda
1 tsp. ground cinnamon
1 tsp. ground cloves
1 tsp. ground allspice

4 cups plain flour (sifted)
1 cup chopped nuts
3 cups fresh apples
(simmered in water until
just tender) or one 8-oz. pkg.
dried apples (prepared according
to directions on pkg.)

Preheat oven to 325⁰. Cream butter and sugar with electric mixer. Mix all other ingredients with wooden spoon, so the apples won't be mushy. Add soda to apples and mix in. Sift spices together with flour and add. Then add remaining ingredients. Bake in a greased and floured tube pan about 1 hour and 20 minutes at 325⁰. This cake is particularly good at Christmas time. It makes a beautiful gift for a friend. It keeps for months in the refrigerator or freezer.

Mrs. Lawrence R. Dixon, III
Florence

FRESH APPLE CAKE

2½ cups flour
2 cups sugar
1 tsp. cinnamon
2 tsp. baking powder
1 tsp. salt

4 eggs
1½ cups cooking oil
1 tsp. vanilla
3 cups chopped apples
1 cup chopped pecans

Mix all dry ingredients. Add eggs. Slowly pour in cooking oil, beating constantly. Add vanilla. Fold in apples and nuts. Pour into tube pan which has been greased and bake one hour at 350^0.

Topping

1½ cups brown sugar
½ cup chopped nuts

1 stick butter
3 tsp. milk

Place all ingredients in saucepan, bring to a boil. Cook until soft ball stage and pour onto cake while warm.

Mrs. R. L. Anderson
Travelers Rest

FRESH APPLE CAKE

3 cups diced apples
1 cup cooking oil
1½ tsp. salt
1½ cups brown sugar
2 well-beaten eggs

1 cup golden seedless raisins
1 cup chopped nuts
2 tsp. vanilla
1 tsp. orange extract
3 cups all-purpose flour

Mix apples and brown sugar and let stand for 30 minutes. Add other ingredients and blend well. Cook in well-greased and floured tube pan at 275^0 for 1½ hours or until cake loosens at sides.

Ann M. Aycock
Jonesville

APRICOT CAKE

1 box Pillsbury Yellow Cake Mix
½ cup sugar
½ cup oil

1 cup apricot nectar
4 eggs

Blend mix, sugar, oil and enough nectar to moisten. Add eggs one at a time beating thoroughly each time. Add remaining nectar and continue beating for 3 minutes. Bake one hour at 325⁰ in a well greased bundt pan, or until when touched springs back. Glaze while hot with 2 cups powdered sugar and juice of two lemons.

Mrs. Randy Morris
Sandy Springs

BERRIES AND CREAM CAKE

1 1/3 cups (15 oz. cans) Eagle Brand
   sweetened condensed milk
1/3 cup lemon juice
1 Tbs. grated lemon rind

1 pint fresh strawberries
   (quartered)
1 cup heavy cream
8 ladyfingers (8 oz. pkg.)

In medium sized bowl, combine first 3 ingredients. Fold in berries. Whip ½ cup cream until stiff. Fold into Eagle Brand mixture. Split ladyfingers. Line a 9x5x3 inch loaf pan. Pour berry mixture into pan, keeping ladyfingers in place. Refrigerate until firm (at least 3 hours). To remove cake, run spatula around inside of cake pan. Invert pan on plate. Whip remaining cream (½ cup) until stiff. Spread on top and sides of cake.

Mrs. William W. Doar, Jr.
Georgetown

CINNAMON CARROT CAKE

2 cups sifted flour
2 cups sugar
2 tsp. soda
2 tsp. salt
2 tsp. cinnamon

1¼ cups cooking oil
3 cups grated raw carrots
4 eggs
1 cup nuts (pecans or black walnuts)

Mix all dry ingredients, then add oil, carrots, and eggs. Bake at 350⁰ for 35 minutes or until done.

Icing

1-8 oz. pkg. cream cheese
1 lb. box confectioners' sugar
1 cup pecans or walnuts

½ stick butter (melted)
2 tsp. vanilla

Mix and spread.

Mrs. R. L. Stevenson
Greenville

CARROT CAKE

3 cups sifted flour	2 cups sugar
2 tsp. baking powder	1¼ cups corn oil
2 tsp. baking soda	1 tsp. vanilla
2 tsp. cinnamon	4 large eggs
½ tsp. salt	3 cups finely grated
1 cup raisins	(shredded) raw carrots
1 cup coarsely chopped	
black walnuts	

On wax paper sift together the flour, baking powder, baking soda, cinnamon and salt. On another piece of wax paper mix together the raisins and walnuts. Use 2 Tbs. of the sifted flour mixture and toss with raisins and walnuts. In a large mixing bowl, beat together the sugar, oil and vanilla; thoroughly beat in eggs, one at a time. Stir in sifted dry ingredients in several additions, alternately with carrots, and blend batter just until smooth after each addition. Stir in floured raisin-walnut mixture. Turn into greased angel cake pan (10 x 3 inches); batter will not come up high in pan after baking. Bake in a preheated moderate (350⁰) oven until top springs back when lightly touched with finger-about 1¼ hours. Place on wire rack to cool in pan for 10 minutes. Turn out on wire rack: turn right side up. Cool. Spread top with Cream Cheese Frosting. Note: In measuring the carrot, shake it down in the measuring cup but do not pack it tightly. To make the 3 cups of carrot called for, 6 medium size carrots (pared) will be needed.

Cream Cheese Frosting

1 pkg. (3 oz.) cream cheese, soft	2¼ cups sifted confectioners' sugar
2 Tbs. light corn syrup	½ tsp. vanilla

In a medium mixing bowl, stir together until blended the cream cheese and light corn syrup. Gradually stir in the sifted confectioners' sugar, then the vanilla, keeping smooth. Makes enough frosting for top of Carrot Cake baked in 10-inch Angel-cake pan. Note: If you wish to frost the whole cake, just double the above recipe.

Mrs. Myrtie Thomason Patrick

MOTHER'S PINEAPPLE CAKE

2½ cups sifted cake flour
3½ tsp. baking powder,
   double acting
1 tsp. salt
1 2/3 cups sugar
2/3 cups shortening

¾ cup shortening
¾ cup milk
3 eggs (unbeaten)
1½ tsp. vanilla extract
½ cup pineapple juice

Sift dry ingredients together (cake flour, baking powder, salt, and sugar). Put dry ingredients, shortening, and milk in mixing bowl and mix all at once at medium speed for 2 minutes. Add 3 eggs (unbeaten), beating well after each addition. Also, add ½ cup pineapple juice and 1½ tsp. vanilla. Mix eggs, pineapple juice, and vanilla for a total of 3 minutes at medium speed. Bake in 3 greased and floured 9-inch cake pans at 350⁰ for 18 minutes.

Filling for Pineapple Cake

1½ boxes light brown sugar
1 (20 oz.) can crushed pineapple

¾ cup water

Mix sugar with ¾ cup water and boil until sugar coats spoon. Add drained pineapple and cook until it is thick enough to spread. Then add 1 Tbs. of butter. Cool mixture before putting between layers and on top and sides of layers.

Mrs. Allen B. Thomas
Aiken

CARROT-PINEAPPLE CAKE

2 cups sifted self-rising flour
2 tsp. cinnamon
1½ cups cooking (salad) oil
2 cups sugar
4 eggs

2 cups finely grated
  carrots
1 (8¼ oz.) can crushed
  pineapple
¼ cup chopped nuts

Heat oven to 325⁰. Grease thoroughly and lightly dust with flour two 9-inch square pans. Sift flour and cinnamon together. Combine oil, sugar, and eggs in a large mixer bowl and beat thoroughly. Add flour mixture and beat to blend ingredients. Fold in carrots, pineapple, and nuts. Pour batter into prepared pans and bake until cake begins to pull away from sides of pan (about 1 hour). Cool 15 minutes and remove from pan. Cool completely before frosting. Note: If using plain flour, add 2 tsp. baking powder, 1½ tsp. soda, and 1 tsp. salt to flour.

Cream Cheese Icing

1 (8 oz.) pkg. cream cheese
1 stick (½ cup) butter
   or margarine

1 box (1 lb.) confectioners' sugar
2 tsp. vanilla extract

Combine all ingredients and beat to blend. Spread on cake. This is a lot of icing, but this amount is delicious with this cake. For a smaller cake the icing recipe may be cut in half.

Mrs. Jean S. Wooten
Lexington

PEACH PINWHEEL BUTTER CAKE

½ cup (1 stick) butter
1¼ cups sugar
2 eggs
½ tsp. almond extract
2½ cups sifted cake flour
2 tsp. baking powder

½ tsp. cinnamon
¼ tsp. salt
¼ tsp. nutmeg
1/9 tsp. ginger
¾ cup milk

Line two pans with wax paper. Cream butter and sugar until light and fluffy. Add eggs, one at a time, beating well after each addition. Add almond extract. Sift together flour, baking powder, cinnamon, salt, nutmeg and ginger. Add to creamed mixture alternately with milk, beginning and ending with dry ingredients. Pour batter into pans; bake 25-30 minutes at 350⁰. Let stand 10 minutes, then remove from pans onto wire racks. Cool completely before frosting with Peach Icing.

Peach Icing

1 cup sliced fresh peaches
2 tsp. lemon juice
¼ cup finley diced fresh
  peaches
¼ cup firmly packed
  light brown sugar

½ cup (1 stick) butter
½ tsp. almond extract
3 cups confectioners' sugar
Slivered almonds

Dip sliced peaches in lemon juice; drain on paper towels. In a small mixing bowl, combine diced peaches and brown sugar. Beat until sugar is completely dissolved. Add butter. Beat until light and fluffy. Add almond extract. Gradually add confectioner's sugar. Place bottom cake layer on cake plate. Spread on ¼ of the icing and cover with a layer of sliced peaches. Spread ¼ of the icing over bottom of second cake layer and place this side on top of peaches. Frost top with remaining icing. Decorate with peach slices and almonds to form pinwheel.

Mrs. Nancy Carter
De Ridder, Louisiana

PRUNE CAKE

2 cups sugar	3 eggs
2 cups self-rising flour	1 cup cooking oil
1 tsp. cinnamon	1 jar junior baby food prune
1 tsp. nutmeg	with Tapioca
1 tsp. all-spice	1 cup nuts

Mix sugar, flour and spices, add cooking oil and prune, eggs one at a time and nuts. Put in tube pan. Bake at 325⁰ for 1 hour.

Mrs. Belle Scott
Clinton

STRAWBERRY CAKE

2¼ cups flour (plain or cake flour)	1½ cups sugar
2 tsp. baking powder	¾ cup crushed strawberries
½ tsp. salt	2 eggs
½ cup butter	
1 tsp. vanilla	

Mix butter, sugar, eggs, salt, baking powder, then add flour and strawberries. Makes two 9 inch layers. Bake at 350⁰ for 25 minutes.

Frosting

1 box powdered sugar	4 Tbs. margarine (if too thick
½ cup mashed strawberries	to please, add lemon juice)

Mrs. H. B. (Verna) Bateman
Columbia

33

SUMMER FRUIT CAKE

1 cup butter or margarine	1 lb. dates, chopped
2 cups sugar	1 can angel flake coconut
4 eggs	(optional)
1 tsp. soda	2 cups nuts
½ cup buttermilk	1 lb. candy orange slices
3½ cups flour	(gum drops) chopped

Cream butter and sugar, add eggs one at a time, beat well. Dissolve soda in buttermilk and add. Roll nuts, candy and dates in flour and add (also coconut if using). Put into one 9 x 15 inch pan or two 8 x 8 inch pans. Bake at 250⁰ for 2½ hours.

Topping

1 cup orange juice	2 cups confectioners' sugar

Mix well and pour slowly over hot cake. Let stand in pan overnight before serving. Can be frozen.

Mrs. Rufus D. Elliott
Chattanooga, Tennessee

WHITE FRUIT CAKE

12 eggs	½ lb. citron
1¼ lbs. butter	1½ lbs. cherries
1½ lbs. (3 cups) sugar	(½ red, ½ green)
6 cups flour	3 lbs. raisins (white)
1 lb. candied pineapple	1 lb. mixed fruit
1 small coconut or	1 small pkg. almonds
1 (14 oz.) pkg. Baker's	1 small pkg. English
Angle Flake Coconut	walnuts
1 tsp. nutmeg	

Mix pineapple, coconut, citron, cherries, raisins, and the mixed fruit together with a little flour in a large pan. Add pecans, almonds, and walnuts. Mix well. Cream butter, eggs, sugar, remaining flour, and nutmeg. Pour batter over fruit mixture and mix well. Bake 4 hours at 250⁰ to 275⁰ in well greased pans that are lined with brown paper. Makes 2 large tube-pan size cakes.

Mrs. J. B. Traywick, II
Spartanburg

BLACK NUT CAKE

This cake was the favorite of President Franklin D. Roosevelt. Mrs. Stevens, manager of the Warm Springs Hotel in Warm Springs, Georgia frequently baked this cake for the visiting President. Roosevelt, who described Mrs. Stevens as "Georgia's champion cake baker," would drive from the Little White House to thank her in person whenever she sent him her Black Nut Cake.

1 lb. flour
1 lb. brown sugar
½ lb. country butter
2 qts. shelled pecans
1 Tbs. cooking soda
1 Tbs. cinnamon
1 whole nutmeg (grated)

1 tsp. spice
1 tsp. cloves
1½ lbs. seedless raisins
6 eggs
1 wine glass of wine
   (preferably sherry)
1 tsp. vanilla

Cream butter and sugar together and add one egg at a time and beat until sugar is dissolved. Sift soda into flour, add the mixture, then wine. Add nuts and raisins which have been dredged in flour. Put into a greased steeple-cake pan. Put on top of stove and let steam for one hour. Put cloth over top of boilers to take up moisture, then remove. Put in oven and bake slowly for three hours at 300⁰.

Mrs. James S. Beaty
Anderson

DATE NUT CAKE

1 lb. dates
½ lb. cherries
1 lb. nuts
1 cup flour

4 eggs
1 cup sugar
Rum flavoring

Mix flour and sugar with dates, nuts, and cherries. Beat eggs and pour them over this mixture. Mix and bake in 2 loaf pans at 250⁰ for 1 to 1½ hours.

Mrs. Bill (Louise) Lawrence
Florence

PECAN UPSIDE-DOWN CAKE

¼ cup butter
¼ cup brown sugar
1 tsp. water
1 cup broken pecans
1 cup cake flour
1½ tsp. baking powder

1/8 tsp. salt
2 eggs (separated)
1 cup granulated sugar
6 Tbs. hot water
1 tsp. vanilla

Melt butter in pan, stir in brown sugar and water, remove from heat, arrange pecans in rows. Cool. Sift together flour, baking powder and salt. Beat egg yolks until thick. Gradually beat in sugar. Mix in hot water and vanilla, add to flour mixture. Fold in stiffly beaten egg whites. Pour batter over nut mixture. Bake in moderately slow oven at 325⁰ for about 1 hour. Let stand about 5 minutes after removing from oven. Turn upside down on plate.

Mrs. James M. Graham
Hartsville

CHOC-CHIP CAKE

1 (8 oz.) cream cheese
1 unbeaten egg
1/3 cup sugar
1/8 tsp. salt
1 (6 oz.) pkg. unsweetened
  chocolate chips
1½ cups flour
1 cup sugar

¼ cup cocoa
1 tsp. soda
½ tsp. salt
1 cup water
1/3 cup oil
1 tsp. vinegar
1 tsp. vanilla

Combine cream cheese, egg, sugar, and salt. Beat well. Stir in chocolate chips. Sift flour, sugar, soda and salt. Add to flour mixture water, oil, vinegar, and vanilla. Beat well. Pour into greased square or round pan. Top with cheese mixture. Bake at 350⁰ for 50 minutes. We love it!

Mrs. Isadore Lourie
Columbia

COCONUT CAKE

3 cups self-rising flour	2 sticks butter
2 cups sugar	2 cups milk
4 eggs	1 tsp. vanilla extract

Cream butter and sugar well. Add eggs one at a time. Add flour and milk alternately. (Do not over beat). Stir in vanilla flavoring. Makes 4 layers. Grease and flour 9-inch cake pans. Bake at 325^0 for 20 to 25 minutes or until layers test done.

Frosting

3 cups sugar	1 fresh coconut, grated
¼ stick butter	1 small can angel flake coconut
1 pint cream (whipping)	to beautify outside of cake
½ tsp. vanilla extract	

Bring sugar and cream to a boil. Add coconut and vanilla and butter. Boil until creamy and white (about 12 minutes). Do not over cook. Let cool before spreading between layers. Save enough for top and sides and beautify with angel flake coconut.

Mrs. Allen B. Thomas
Aiken

COFFEE CAKE

1 box yellow cake mix	1 cup pecans (chopped)
1 small box instant vanilla	1 Tbs. vanilla flavoring
pudding	1 tsp. butter flavoring
¾ cup liquid corn oil	½ cup sugar
¾ cup water	4 Tbs. cinnamon
4 eggs	

Topping

1½ cups powdered sugar	1 tsp. butter flavoring
1 tsp. vanilla flavoring	Small amount milk

Combine first 4 ingredients. Then one egg at a time. Add flavoring and beat for 8 minutes. Add 1 cup of pecans. Into a loaf pan pour a thin layer of batter. Mix sugar and cinnamon and sprinkle over batter. Alternate batter and sugar-cinnamon mixture—ending with batter. Bake in 350^0 oven for 35 to 40 minutes. Combine all topping ingredients with small amount of milk. Spread on cake while hot.

Catha W. Reid
West Columbia

EASY COFFEE CAKE

¼ cup butter
1 cup sugar
2 egg yolks
2 egg whites
½ cup milk

1½ cups flour
4 tsp. baking powder
½ tsp. vanilla or
1 tsp. lemon extract
½ tsp. salt

Cream butter well, adding sugar gradually. Add egg yolks and beat thoroughly. Sift flour and measure. Resift with dry ingredients. Add alternately with the milk to the creamed mixture. Beat egg whites stiff and fold into creamed mixture. Add flavoring. Pour into greased pan (7½ x 11 x 1½ inches). Cover with strudel and bake 25 minutes at 375⁰.

Strudel

1 cup sugar
3 tsp. cinnamon

¼ cup flour
¼ cup melted butter

Blend together with a fork. This may be put into refrigerator overnight and baked in the morning.

Mrs. Allen B. Thomas
Aiken

MRS. WHITE'S COFFEE CAKE

1½ cups sifted cake flour
¼ cup butter
½ cup sugar
1 egg

Grated rind of 1 lemon
½ tsp. nutmeg
1½ tsp. baking powder
½ cup milk

Cream butter and sugar. Add egg and beat until fluffy. Mix in lemon rind. Sift flour, nutmeg and baking powder together, and add alternately with milk. Pour about half the batter over the bottom of a well-greased pan. Then sprinkle filling over it and pour remaining batter over the top. Bake in moderate oven 375⁰ for 35 to 40 minutes, or until cake tests done. When cool cut into squares and serve.

Filling

1½ Tbs. melted butter	¼ tsp. cinnamon
½ cup brown sugar	½ cup chopped pecans
1 Tbs. flour	

Mix butter and sugar. Add flour, cinnamon and nutmeats. Use as directed above. Makes 12 pieces; 218 calories per serving. Preparation time, 55 minutes.

Mrs. James Benjamin White
Winnsboro

SOUR CREAM COFFEE CAKE

1½ sticks butter (or margarine)	1 tsp. baking powder
2 cups sugar	½ tsp. salt
1 cup sour cream	1 cup chopped pecans
2 eggs, well-beaten	3 Tbs. dark brown sugar
1 tsp. vanilla	1 tsp. ground cinnamon
2 cups all-purpose flour, sifted twice	

Cream butter, sugar and sour cream. Add eggs, one at a time, and vanilla and beat well. Combine dry ingredients and add to creamed mixture, beat well. Thoroughly grease a 10-inch bundt or tube pan. Make filling by combining chopped nuts, brown sugar and cinnamon. Put half of cake batter in pan then sprinkle with all of the filling, adding remainder of batter next. Bake at 350⁰ for 45 minutes or until done. Let cake cool before turning out. Drizzle glaze over top of cake while still warm.

Glaze

1 cup confectioners' sugar	2 Tbs. condensed milk

Ann Traynham
Columbia

COCA-COLA CAKE

2 cups sugar	1½ cups small marshmallows
2 cups flour	1 tsp. soda
½ cup oleo	1 tsp. vanilla
½ cup shortening	2 beaten eggs
3 Tbs. cocoa	½ cup buttermilk
½ cup Coca-Cola	

Sift sugar and flour together in mixing bowl. Place oleo, shortening, cocoa, and Coca-Cola in saucepan, bring to a boil, and add flour and sugar. Then add marshmallows, vanilla, eggs, and buttermilk. Add soda. Beat well, pour in greased and floured pan (13 x 9 x 2 inches).

Icing

½ cup oleo	1 tsp. vanilla
3 Tbs. Coca-Cola	1 cup marshmallows
¾ lb. box powdered sugar	1 cup chopped nuts

Bring oleo and Coca-Cola to boil. Add other ingredients. Pour on cake in pan while both cake and icing are hot.

Mrs. Beverley Sanders
Sumter

COCA-COLA CAKE

1½ cups sugar	½ cup shortening
1½ cups miniature marshmallows	1 cup Coca-Cola
2 cups plain flour	½ cup buttermilk
1 stick margarine	2 eggs (well beaten)
3 Tbs. cocoa	1 tsp. soda

Mix sugar, marshmallows, and flour in bowl. In saucepan, bring margarine, cocoa, shortening, and Coca-Cola to a boil. Pour over dry ingredients until marshmallows are almost melted. Add buttermilk, eggs and soda. Mix well, but do not beat. Pour into well-greased and floured oblong pan (9x12 inches) and bake in 350⁰ oven for 35 to 40 minutes.

Icing

1 stick margarine
6 Tbs. Coca-Cola
3 Tbs. cocoa

1 box powdered sugar
1 cup nuts (chopped)

Bring to boil margarine, Coca-Cola, and cocoa. Remove from heat and add powdered sugar. Beat until smooth. Add chopped nuts. Pour over hot cake.

Mrs. Wm. Jennings Bryan Dorn
Greenwood

POUND CAKE

3 cups sugar
3 cups all-purpose flour
6 eggs

½ lb. butter
½ pint whipping cream
2 tsp. vanilla extract

Cream butter and sugar, adding eggs to mixture one at a time. Add other ingredients and pour into greased 10-inch tube pan. For easy removal of cake, cut a circle of waxpaper to go into the bottom of cake pan. Put cake in cold oven and turn temperature to 350^0. Bake 1 hour and 10 minutes. Test cake for doneness.

Mrs. Allen B. Thomas
Aiken

PEARL POUND CAKE

2 sticks margarine
½ cup shortening
1 cup milk
3 cups sugar

3 cups flour
1 tsp. baking powder
5 large eggs
Use any flavoring you like

Cream margarine and shortening well; add sugar gradually, then eggs one at a time, beating well after each addition. Add baking powder to flour and add alternately with milk to creamed mixture. Bake at 320^0 for about 1 hour and 20 minutes. Let cool in pan.

Mrs. M. P. Ferris
Georgetown

41

CRUSTY POUND CAKE

¾ lb. butter (3 sticks)   1 Tbs. vanilla & 1 tsp. almond
3 cups sugar   or lemon
6 eggs   1 tsp. salt
                               3 cups flour (measure before sifting)

Cream butter with sugar until it is a fine mealy mixture. Add eggs one at a time and beat mixture after each egg. Then add vanilla and almond or lemon flavoring. Then add flour and salt slowly to the mixture. Then beat mixture until it is creamy smooth. Preheat oven to 350^0. Bake cake at 350^0 for one hour without opening the oven door, then bake for 30 minutes at 325^0. Use tube cake pan for baking cake. Line bottom of pan with waxpaper, grease pan, and flour it.

Mrs. Hazel Martin
West Columbia

PINEAPPLE POUND CAKE

½ cup shortening   1 tsp. baking powder
½ cup butter (2 sticks)   ¼ cup milk
2¾ cups sugar   1 tsp. vanilla
6 eggs   ¾ cup undrained crushed
3 cups flour   pineapple, with juice

Cream shortening, butter and sugar. Add eggs, one at a time, beating thoroughly after each addition. Add flour sifted with baking powder, one spoonful at a time, alternately with milk. Add vanilla, stir in crushed pineapple and juice and blend well. Pour batter into well greased and floured 10-inch tube pan. Place in cold oven. Bake at 325^0 for 1 hour or until top springs back when touched lightly.

Topping

¼ cup butter (½ stick)   1 cup drained crushed
1½ cups powdered sugar   pineapple

Combine ingredients and pour over cake while hot.

Mrs. R. L. Anderson
Travelers Rest

FRESH APPLE POUND CAKE

2 cups sugar	1½ cups cooking oil
4 eggs	3 cups plain flour
1 tsp. baking soda	1 tsp. salt
1 tsp. vanilla	3 cups apples, diced
1 cup chopped pecans	1 cup coconut

Mix sugar and oil. Add eggs one at a time and beat after each. Sift soda, salt with flour. Add to egg mixture; beat well. Add apples, nuts, coconut and vanilla. Bake in greased and floured tube pan 1 hour and 20 minutes at 325⁰. Do not open oven.

Icing

1½ cups brown sugar	½ cup chopped nuts
1 stick butter or margarine	3 tsp. milk

Place all ingredients in saucepan, bring to a boil. Cook until soft ball stage and pour on cake while warm. Cake is almost as good without topping.

Mrs. Paul B. Agnew
Orangeburg

HALF-POUND CAKE

½ lb. country butter	½ tsp. vanilla
2 scant cups of sugar	½ tsp. almond
5 large eggs	¼ tsp. salt
2 cups sifted all-purpose flour	

Cream butter thoroughly at room temperature. Add sugar gradually until quite fluffy. Add one egg at a time and beat well with each addition. Measure extract into the broken egg. Add flour, to which a pinch (¼ tsp.) of salt has been added and sifted. Beat well. Use waxpaper in bottom of pan. Grease the paper and stem of the pan. Fill pan 2/3 full. Set oven at 350⁰ and bake one hour. Remove from oven and leave cake in pan for 10 minutes. Run knife around edge to loosen. Turn out and let cool. Note well—start cake in cold oven.

Ann M. Aycock
Jonesville

IDA ROGERS' WHIPPING CREAM POUND CAKE

½ lb. soft creamery butter
3 cups sugar
6 eggs
3 cups flour

½ pt. whipping cream
 (not whipped)
1 Tbs. vanilla
Pinch of salt

Cream butter and sugar well. Add eggs one at a time. Add salt Add alternately flour and whipping cream, beginning with flour and ending with flour. Add vanilla. Grease and flour tube pan or bundt pan. Put cake mixture in cold oven. Set temperature at 325^0 and bake 1¼ hours. Set cake on rack for 10 minutes to cool before removing cake from pan.

Mrs. Frances Peebles Byars
Easley

SARAH'S POUND CAKE

4 cups sifted cake flour
1 tsp. baking powder
1 cup shortening

1 cup butter
2 cups eggs
3 cups sugar

With electric mixer, cream cake flour and baking powder with butter and shortening. In separate bowl beat (with fork) the eggs while adding sugar. Add egg—sugar mixture to creamed mixture. Beat until well mixed. Pour into a greased and floured 10-inch tube pan. Bake at 250^0 for ½ hour and then bake at 300^0 for an additional hour.

Mrs. Craig Stephens
Dillon

20TH CENTURY POUND CAKE

4 cups all-purpose flour
 (well-sifted) not self-rising
2 cups sugar
1 cup creamery butter
1 cup buttermilk

1 tsp. pure vanilla extract
1 tsp. pure lemon extract
½ tsp. baking soda

44

Cream butter and sugar well, add eggs, one at a time, beating constantly between each egg. Add flour and milk alternately until all this is well-mixed and smooth. Put into a greased, prepared pan (one with a steeple is best). Bake in a moderate oven 350⁰ for 1½ hours.

Ann M. Aycock
Jonesville

WALNUT POUND CAKE

½ lb. butter
½ cup shortening
5 eggs
3 cups plain flour
1 tsp. baking powder

1 tsp. vanilla
½ tsp. rum flavoring
1 cup cream (or half-and-half)
1 cup walnuts (chopped fine)

Cream butter and shortening, add sugar and beat well. Add eggs, one at a time, beating well. Add flavoring and beat. Mix ¼ cup flour with nuts. Add remaining flour and baking powder alternately with milk, starting and ending with flour. Fold in nuts. Bake in large greased and floured tube pan (bundt pan preferred) for 1 hour and 20 minutes at 325⁰. Do not open oven during first hour of baking.

Miss Lillian Watson
Mullins

BUTTER NUT CAKE

1 cup shortening
2 cups sugar
4 eggs
1 cup sweet milk

2½ cups cake flour (or plain)
½ cup self-rising flour
¾ Tbs. butter nut flavoring

Cream shortening and sugar for 10 minutes at high speed. Add eggs one at a time. Add milk and flour alternately. Bake in a tube pan at 325⁰ for 1 hour.

Mrs. Belle Scott
Clinton

45

GYPSY CAKE

This is an old Abbeville recipe traditionally served as a dessert after Christmas Day dinner. As familiar as the gleeful shouts of "Merry Christmas" and the laughter of children opening gifts was the "wsh-wsh" sound of the old hand-wrought syllabub churn. Below are the recipes for the various parts of the Gypsy Cake (or as some call similar desserts, "Tipsy Cake").

Sponge Cake

10 eggs	3 cups flour
2 cups sugar	

Beat the whites and yellows of eggs separately. Mix sugar in yellows and fold in the whites. Finally, fold in the flour. Bake in ungreased steeple pan at 325^0 for about one hour.

Boiled Custard

1 qt. milk	4 eggs
1 cup sugar	1 tsp. vanilla

Beat eggs. Add sugar and beat again. In double boiler, scald milk. Slowly add egg mixture, and cook slowly until thick. Add vanilla.

Syllabub

1 qt. whipping cream	Sugar to taste
1 cup milk	Flavor to taste with sherry

Churn with syllabub churn. Allow froth to drain before putting on top of Gypsy Cake. Line large bowl with slices of sponge cake, adorn with slivered almonds, and sprinkle with sherry. Cover cake with boiled custard and fill to top of bowl. Top with syllabub.

Mrs. Sarah Perrin Cox
Abbeville

MORAVIAN SUGAR CAKE

Especially appropriate for Easter breakfast or any brunch.

1 cup hot mashed potatoes	1 pkg. yeast
1 scant cup sugar	½ cup lukewarm water
½ cup shortening	½ Tbs. sugar
¼ cup soft butter	1 cup potato water
1½ tsp. salt	2 beaten eggs
6 to 8 cups sifted plain flour	½ tsp. nutmeg

Butter, brown sugar, cream, and cinnamon

To the hot, mashed potatoes, add the sugar and shortening, along with the butter and salt. Allow to cool to lukewarm. Dissolve yeast in ½ cup lukewarm potato mixture, along with potato water (water in which potatoes were cooked.) Set aside and allow to rise in warm place until spongy. Add eggs and enough flour to make a soft dough. Allow to rise until double in bulk. Punch down. Spread dough evenly in one greased pan (10 x 15 inches) and three pans (8 inches) and let rise again. When dough is light, punch holes in dough with fingers, about 1½ inches apart all over. Fill holes with soft butter and sprinkle tops generously with brown sugar (1 lb. box). Bake at 375^0 until lightly browned (about 20 minutes). Remove and dribble a little cream or canned milk and return to oven for several minutes. Take from oven and dust with cinnamon. Freeze well.

Mrs. Judith C. Robinson
Clover

VANILLA WAFER CAKE

2 cups sugar	12 oz. box vanilla wafers,
2 sticks butter	crushed
6 eggs	1½ cups chopped nuts
½ cup milk	1 can coconut

Cream sugar and butter. Add eggs, milk and crushed vanilla wafers. Add nuts and the coconut. Bake at 250^0 for about 2 hours, or until done.

Miss Lillian Watson
Mullins

MY MOTHER'S ONE, TWO, THREE, FOUR CAKE

1 cup butter	4 eggs
2 cups sugar	1 tsp. vanilla
3 cups sifted flour	1 cup sweet milk

Cream butter and sugar until smooth. Alternately add milk, eggs, and flour, beating smooth after each addition. Add vanilla and stir until smooth. Pour into 2 large greased and floured cake pans and bake at 350⁰ for 25 to 30 minutes. Fill with favorite filling.

Cooked Pineapple Frosting

1 large can crushed pineapple	1/8 lb. butter
1 cup sugar	2 egg yolks

Drain off ¾ of a small glass of pineapple juice. Add sugar and cook slowly for about 15 minutes. Add butter and 2 egg yolks. Cook slowly about 10 minutes until thick. Spread between layers. Frost top with seven-minute frosting. (See below.)

Seven-Minute Frosting

2 egg whites	2 tsp. light corn syrup
1½ cups sugar	1 tsp. vanilla or
1/3 cup water	½ tsp. almond extract

Combine unbeaten egg whites, sugar, water, and corn syrup in top of double boiler. Beat just enough to blend ingredients. Place over rapidly boiling water and beat with hand or electric mixer until light and fluffy and it holds its shape (about 7 minutes). Add vanilla or almond. Continue beating until frosting stands in peaks. Frost top of cake.

Mrs. Ernest L. (Elizabeth) Cook
Hartsville

QUEEN ELIZABETH CAKE

1 small pkg. chopped dates	1 egg
1 tsp. soda	1½ cups sifted flour
1 cup sugar	½ tsp. salt
¼ cup oleo	1 tsp. baking powder

Boil 1 cup water and pour over dates. Add soda and simmer for several minutes. Set aside. Mix remaining ingredients together and mix alternately with date mixture. Pour cake mixture into greased loaf or rectangle pan. Bake 1 hour or until done.

Icing

10 Tbs. brown sugar	10 Tbs. butter
10 Tbs. canned milk	1 cup nuts

Boil 5 minutes and beat. Then add 1 cup chopped nuts.

Mrs. V. L. Durham
Columbia

RED VELVET CAKE

½ cup shortening	2¼ cups cake flour
2 eggs	1 cup buttermilk
1½ cups sugar	1 tsp. soda (sift before mixing)
2 oz. red cake coloring	1 Tbs. vinegar
2 Tbs. cocoa	1 Tbs. vanilla
½ tsp. salt	

Cream shortening and sugar, add eggs. Mix cocoa and cake coloring together, add to above, add vanilla, sift flour and salt, and add alternately with buttermilk. Fold in soda and vinegar. Bake at 300⁰ for 20-30 minutes.

Frosting

Cream 2 sticks butter, 1 tsp. vanilla, 1 cup granulated sugar. Mix until fluffy. Cook 1 cup water and 2 Tbs. corn starch until thick. Cool. Add cream base and beat well until like whipped cream.

Mrs. Fred R. Tinsley
Columbia

OATMEAL CAKE

1 cup oatmeal	1 cup white sugar
1 stick butter	1 tsp. nutmeg
1¼ cups boiling water	1 tsp. cinnamon
2 eggs (beaten)	1 1/3 cups flour
1 tsp. soda	Dash of salt
1 cup brown sugar	

Place oatmeal in bowl with butter on top. Pour 1¼ cups boiling water over this and leave for 20 minutes. While waiting, mix other ingredients, then pour into first mixture. Stir and pour into greased and floured pan. Bake for 35 minutes at 350⁰ .

Icing

1 cup brown sugar	1 cup coconut
1 stick butter (melted)	1 cup pecans
¼ cup milk	1 tsp. vanilla

Stir sugar, butter, and milk together and add coconut, pecans, and vanilla. Pour over top of cake and broil for a moment until topping begins to brown.

Mrs. Beverley Sanders
Sumter

 SPICE CAKE WITH BAKED ICING

1 cup margarine	2 cups brown sugar
2 eggs–plus 2 egg yolks	1 tsp. baking soda
(save whites for frosting)	1 tsp. ground cloves
2-2/3 cups cake flour	1 tsp. cinnamon
1 cup sour milk	

If sour milk not available you can add 1 teaspoon vinegar or lemon juice to milk.

Cream margarine and brown sugar, add eggs one at a time, beating well after each. Add sifted cake flour alternating with sour milk, beat, add all other ingredients, mixing well. Pour into large (12x15x3 inches) pan, which has been greased and floured. Spread with icing.

Icing

2 egg whites   1 cup brown sugar
½ cup chopped pecans

Beat egg whites until soft peaks form, gradually add brown sugar, beating until stiff, then fold in pecans and spread over cake batter. Place in preheated oven and bake 40 to 60 minutes at 325⁰.

Mrs. Roy E. Riddle
Anderson

DEVIL'S FOOD FUDGE SQUARES

2 cups plain flour   4 Tbs. cocoa
2 cups sugar   1 tsp. soda
Pinch salt   ½ cup buttermilk
½ cup butter or margarine   2 eggs
½ cup solid shortening   1 Tbs. vanilla
1 cup water

Sift flour, sugar and salt together in mixing bowl. Melt margarine, shortening, water, and cocoa in a saucepan. Bring to a rapid boil and pour into mixing bowl with dry ingredients. Mix well. Combine soda, buttermilk, eggs and vanilla. Pour into main mixture and beat for about 2 minutes. Pour batter into a greased and floured pan (16 x 11 x 2 inches). Bake in a preheated oven at 325⁰ for about 30 minutes.

Mary Brigman
Conway

BLACK BOTTOM CUPS

1½ cups flour
1 cup sugar
¼ cup cocoa
1 tsp. soda
½ tsp. salt

1 cup water
1/3 cup cooking oil
1 Tbs. vinegar
1 tsp. vanilla

Mix dry ingredients together. Add remaining ingredients and beat until well blended. Fill lined muffin cups 1/3 full with batter.

Filling

8 oz. pkg. cream cheese
1 egg
1/3 cup sugar
1/8 tsp. salt

1/8 tsp. salt
1 cup chocolate chips
Chopped nuts

Combine softened cream cheese, egg, sugar and salt; beat well. Stir in chocolate pieces. Place about 1 Tbs. of mixture on batter in each cup. Sprinkle with additional sugar and nuts. Bake at 350⁰ for 30 minutes. Makes 24 cupcakes.

Mrs. Nicholas E. Bosta
Alexandria, Virginia

APPLE CUPCAKES

1 stick oleo
2 eggs
2 cups sugar
2 cups plain flour
1 tsp. soda

1 tsp. baking powder
1 cup chopped pecans
4 cups raw chopped apples
Cinnamon & nutmeg to taste

Cream oleo and sugar. Add eggs and mix well. Add flour, cinnamon, nutmeg, and chopped pecans—and mix well. Fold in chopped raw apples. Line cup cake pans with liners. Fill cups ½ to 2/3 full of batter. Bake approximately 30 minutes in 350⁰ oven. Be sure to use liners in cup cake pans.

Mrs. Emma T. Baker
Sumter

ORANGE CUPCAKES

1 cup sugar	1 tsp. soda
¼ lb. butter	2 cups flour
2 eggs	½ cup raisins
¾ cup buttermilk	½ cup chopped nuts (pecans)

Cream sugar and butter until light. Add eggs one at a time, beating well. (Reserve ¼ cup flour to coat nuts and raisins). Add flour gradually with buttermilk. Use baking cups and bake 20 minutes at 350⁰. Glaze while warm with the following.

Glaze

Juice 2 oranges	Grated rind of 1 orange
Juice 1 lemon	Grated rind of 1 lemon
1 cup sugar	

Heat until sugar has melted and drizzle over cup cakes.

Mrs. Ernest L. (Elizabeth) Cook
Hartsville

Frostings

BUTTER CREAM FROSTING

1 box powdered sugar	3 to 4 Tbs. milk
1 stick soft margarine	1½ tsp. vanilla

Combine ingredients and mix thoroughly.

Mrs. J. W. Waddill
Columbia

CARMEL FROSTING

½ cup butter
1 cup brown sugar
¼ cup sweet milk
1 tsp. vanilla

1¾ cups powdered sugar
½ cup chopped pecans
(optional)

Melt butter. Add brown sugar. Cook over low heat stirring constantly. Add milk. Cook and stir until it comes to a boil. Remove from heat. Cool. Add sifted powdered sugar. Stir until it is of a spreading consistency. Add vanilla, and nuts, if so desired. Recipe frosts a 2 layer cake generously. There's usually some left in the pan for lickin' purposes.

Mrs. John McDonald
Hartsville

COCONUT FROSTING

3 cups sugar
Milk enough to dissolve sugar
1 Tbs. butter

1 grated coconut or 2 pkgs.
frozen grated coconut
1 tsp. lemon juice

Mix sugar and milk. Allow mixture to boil. Add coconut. Cook until thick enough to spread. Remove from heat. Add butter and lemon juice.

Miss Lillian Watson
Mullins

COMFORT ICING

1¾ cups sugar
¾ cup cold water
3 egg whites
1 tsp. baking powder

1 Tbs. lemon juice
1 tsp. vanilla

Boil sugar and water until spins a thread, add gradually a small amount to the stiffly beaten egg whites. Add baking powder and lemon juice. Add remainder of syrup, beat and cook over hot water until frosting becomes slightly grainy around edge of bowl or until it holds its shape. Add vanilla and spread on cake.

Mrs. Doris Herring
Columbia

CREAMY FUDGE ICING

1 stick (½ cup) margarine
4 Tbs. cocoa
1/3 cup evaporated milk

1 Tbs. vanilla
1 cup chopped nuts
1 box 4X confectioners' sugar

Mix first three ingredients by melting margarine over low heat, then adding cocoa and milk. When mixture becomes smooth, remove from heat. Add last three ingredients. Add the sugar last and slowly. If last cup is not needed because mixture becomes to stiff, omit it. The icing can be spread on the cake while it's hot.

Mary Brigman
Conway

PERFECT FUDGE FROSTING

2 oz. semi-sweet chocolate
1 stick butter
1 egg (beaten)
Pinch salt
1 tsp. lemon juice

1½ cups powdered sugar
1 tsp. vanilla
½ tsp. almond extract
1 cup nuts (chopped)

Melt butter and chocolate together. Add egg, sugar, salt, vanilla, and lemon juice. Mix in nuts.

Miss Lillian Watson
Mullins

MINUTE FUDGE FROSTING

½ cup cocoa or 2 blocks chocolate
½ cup sweet milk
½ cup butter or margarine

2 cups sugar
1 tsp. vanilla extract
Pinch salt

Combine all and boil for 3 minutes. Remove from heat and beat until creamy enough to spread. If you like a lighter chocolate frosting put only 6 teaspoonfuls of cocoa.

Mrs. Dalton Gee
Kingstree

55

Cookies

BUTTER COOKIES

1 lb. butter
1 cup sugar
2 egg yolks (beaten)
1 egg white
Rind ½ lemon (grated)
Juice ½ lemon

6 cups flour
1 tsp. baking powder
1 tsp. salt
Coconut, nuts, or
  maraschino cherries

Cream butter until smooth, add sugar, egg yolks, lemon rind. Sift flour, baking powder, salt. Add lemon juice. Mix to smooth dough. Chill several hours. Roll on floured board, brush over top with unbeaten egg white, cut, sprinkle with sugar. Add nuts, coconut, or cherries as topping. Bake 15 minutes.

Mrs. Doris Herring
Columbia

CHOCOLATE CHIP COOKIES

½ cup shortening
¼ cup firmly packed light
  brown sugar
½ cup granulated sugar
1 egg
1 tsp. vanilla flavoring
½ cup chopped pecans

1 cup unsifted all-purpose
  flour
½ tsp. baking soda
½ tsp. salt
1 pkg. (6 oz.) Baker's
  semi-sweet chocolate chips

Beat shortening, sugar, egg, and vanilla until light and fluffy. Blend in flour, soda, and salt; then stir in chips and nuts. Drop by teaspoonfuls, 2 inches apart, onto ungreased baking sheets. Bake at 375⁰ for 8 to 10 minutes, or until lightly browned. Makes about 4 dozen—they keep nicely stored in containers. This recipe may be doubled or tripled.

Miss Mary Ann Armstrong
Chester

DICK'S PECAN COOKIES

2 cups plain flour (sifted)
1½ cups sugar
1 stick margarine (softened)
1 rounded Tbs. shortening
3 eggs (beaten)

1 tsp. vanilla extract
2 tsp. rum extract
2 level tsp. baking powder
1 cup chopped pecans

Preheat oven. Cream sugar, butter, and shortening. Add eggs and beat well. Add flavorings and mix. Sift baking powder with flour and mix well. Add pecans. For crisp cookies, bake at 350° for 14 to 15 minutes. For chewy cookies, bake at 375° for 8 to 10 minutes. Use a teflon cookie sheet or grease a regular cookie sheet.

Mrs. Lawrence R. Dixon, III
Florence

FROZEN ORANGE JUICE COOKIES

1 (12 oz.) box vanilla wafers
1 cup powdered sugar
¼ cup melted margarine
¾ cup chopped pecans

½ cup coconut
1 small can frozen orange
  juice (undiluted)

Mix all ingredients. Roll in small balls. Dust with powdered sugar. These keep real well in the refrigerator and can be frozen.

Mrs. Winfield K. Sharp, III
Anderson

Custards/Puddings

CUSTARD

1 qt. milk
4 eggs beaten

1 cup sugar
1 tsp. vanilla extract

Beat eggs in mixing bowl. Warm milk and sugar in top of double boiler. Pour milk over eggs and return mixture to double boiler. Stir constantly with a wooden spoon until it coats the spoon well. Take off heat and strain into pitcher. Let cool and add vanilla. This custard is delicious over pound cake, and especially over Charlotte Russe, served in a sherbert dish.

Mrs. Hammond A. Harllee
Florence

CHARLOTTE RUSSE

2 rounded Tbs. gelatin	½ cup homemade grape wine
1 pint milk	or purchased brand
1 qt. whipping cream	½ cup powdered sugar (sifted)
1½ tsp. vanilla	Small pinch of salt

Soak gelatin in milk for 10 minutes, then place over moderate heat and stir. Remove from unit as soon as gelatin dissolves. Add salt and allow to cool, stirring occasionally. When fairly thick, beat with mixer until light and spongy. Then fold in the cream, which has been previously whipped, sweetened, and flavored. Pour into molds lined with lady fingers, macaroons, or sponge cake, cut to fit molds. Stand molds in refrigerator until time to serve. Makes 2 quarts. This Charlotte Russe will last several days in refrigerator.

Mrs. Hammond A. Harllee
Florence

PEACH CUSTARD

1 can (1 lb.) peach halves, drained	¼ tsp. cinnamon
	1/8 tsp. cloves
2 1/3 cups milk	4 eggs, slightly beaten
1/3 cup sugar	¼ tsp. vanilla extract
¼ tsp. salt	1/8 tsp. almond extract

Drain peaches, reserving 1 cup syrup. Puree 2-3 peach halves to make 1/3 cup; set aside. Scald milk. Meanwhile, in a small bowl combine sugar, salt, cinnamon and cloves. Blend thoroughly. Add to milk and stir until sugar is dissolved. Gradually add milk mixture to eggs. Add puree, vanilla and almond extract. Pour into 1½-quart shallow baking dish. Set in baking pan on oven rack and pour 1 inch hot water into pan. Bake in preheated 325⁰ oven 60-66 minutes or until a silver knife inserted near center comes out clean. Remove from hot water and cool. Spoon into serving dishes and top with Peach Sauce. Yield: 6-8 servings.

Peach Sauce

1 cup peach syrup
1 Tbs. cornstarch
¼ tsp. almond extract

Gradually add peach syrup to cornstarch. Cook over medium heat, stirring constantly, until mixture thickens and loses starchy taste. Blend in almond extract. Cool and serve over peach custard. Yield: 1 cup.

Mrs. Nancy Carter
De Ridder, Louisiana

BREAD PUDDING

12 slices bread	¾ stick butter
1 egg	Milk (enough to cover bread)
2 Tbs. sugar	Cinnamon

Break up bread into medium size crumbs. Put into casserole dish. Bring milk and butter to a boil. When cool add beaten egg and sugar to milk and butter. Pour over bread crumbs (just to cover). Sprinkle on top with cinnamon and add a little sugar to top. Bake in oven uncovered about 40 minutes or until top is brown.

Mrs. Earle Morris
Columbia

DATE PUDDING

1 cup bread crumbs	1 tsp. baking powder
1 cup sugar	1 cup dates (cut up)
1 cup milk	½ cup chopped nuts
1 egg	

Mix dry ingredients together. Add beaten egg to the milk and mix with the dry ingredients. Add melted butter, dates and nuts. Bake in 350⁰ oven. Serve with whipped cream or ice cream.

Mrs. Frederic S. Otis
Hastings, Nebraska

PINEAPPLE PUDDING

1 pkg. vanilla pudding
  and pie mix

Graham crackers
1 small can crushed pineapple

Mix up pudding mix according to directions on package. Drain pineapple, add to pudding mix while still over heat. Add 1 tablespoon of pineapple juice to mixture on stove. In a dish, put a layer of crackers, then a layer of pudding, then a layer of crackers, then a layer of pudding.

Mrs. Allen B. Thomas
Aiken

MIMI'S ALMOND FLUFF

¾ cup sugar
2 Tbs. flour
¼ tsp. salt
2 cups milk

3 egg whites
3 egg yolks
½ tsp. vanilla
½ tsp. almond flavoring

Mix ½ cup sugar, salt, and flour until smooth. Add milk and cook (in double boiler) over boiling water, stirring constantly until thickened. Add egg yolks gradually, stirring constantly into mixture. Cook 5 minutes. Remove from heat, add vanilla and almond. Cool. Beat together 3 egg whites and ¼ cup sugar until stiff. Gently fold this into first mixture until smooth and fluffy. Serves 6.

Mrs. Randy Morris
Sandy Springs

APPLE SOUFFLE

1 can apple sauce
1 cup sugar
1 cup milk
1 cup Graham cracker
  crumbs

2 eggs
1 stick butter (melted)
Red food coloring
  (if desired)

Mix apple sauce, sugar, milk, cracker crumbs, eggs, butter, and coloring. Pour into baking dish. Cook in 350^0 oven for 45 minutes.

Ruth Ann Collins
Columbia

QUEEN OF PUDDINGS

This favorite recipe from Mount Hope Plantation in Ridgeway appears in the handwriting of my great grandmother from one of the flyleafs of her favorite cookbook. Since she was of French extraction, many of her recipes are of French origin. We always attributed the family's good cooking at both its early Low Country plantations and later at its Up Country homes to the superb combination of French and English backgrounds merged with the native ability of former African slaves to season and cook "just right."

1 pint stale bread crumbs	1 grated lemon rind
1 qt. milk	1 tsp. cream butter
4 eggs (separated)	5 lbs. powdered sugar
1 cup sugar	Juice one lemon
Acid jelly or preserves	

Combine bread crumbs, milk, egg yolks, 1 cup sugar, lemon rind, and butter. Bake at 350⁰. When cool, spread with acid jelly or preserves. Beat egg whites with 5 pounds powdered sugar and lemon juice. Spread over top of pudding, brown quickly.

Charles E. Thomas
Greenville

Fruit

AMBROSIA

Oranges	Coconut
Sugar	

Peel and pare oranges. Remove membrane between sections. Cut into small pieces. Alternate layers of oranges, sugar, and coconut. Top with coconut. Do not stir. Serve with light cake.

Ann M. Aycock
Jonesville

QUICK AMBROSIA

2 large cans crushed pineapple
2 (6 oz.) cans frozen undiluted
  orange juice
1 pkg. frozen coconut

¾ cup sugar
6 bananas
Cherries

Mix all ingredients and refrigerate overnight.

Mrs. Belle Scott
Clinton

AVOCADO MOUSSE

1 Tbs. gelatin (dissolved
  in 2 Tbs. water)
1 pkg. lime jello
2 cups hot water
1 cup ripe avocado
  (mashed)
½ cup mayonnaise

½ cup cream (whipped)
Strawberries, pineapple sticks,
  white grapes, and Bing cherries
Pecans
Orange peel

Dissolve gelatin mixture and jello in hot water; when partially congealed, stir in remaining ingredients. Pour into a mold greased with mayonnaise. Allow to set in refrigerator. Unmold on lettuce, garnish with fresh strawberries, pineapple sticks, white grapes, and Bing cherries. Fill center of ring with mayonnaise combined with pecans and grated orange peel. Serve with ham, a cheese souffle, and hot rolls. Serves 8.

Mrs. Clement F. Haynsworth, Jr.
Greenville

BAKED FRUIT CASSEROLE

3 oranges
1 (no. 2) can pineapple
  (cut in quarters)
1 (no. 2) can pear halves
  (cut)
1 (no. 2) can sliced peaches

1 small jar maraschino cherries
1 stick butter or margarine
2/3 cup sugar
¼ tsp. salt
1/3 cup sherry
2 cups water

Slice oranges thin, cut in quarters, remove peel. Grind peel, boil 20 minutes in water. Discard water. Cut orange pieces small. Add drained peel to cut orange and canned fruits. Melt butter and make paste with sugar, flour and salt. Cook until thickened, add sherry. Butter large casserole. Arrange fruits, mixing them. Pour sauce over, bake at 375^0 for 20 minutes. Serve with turkey, ham or chicken. Serves 10 to 12.

Mrs. Clement F. Haynsworth, Jr.
Greenville

FRUIT SALAD DESSERT

4 pkgs. black cherry jello
1 cup crushed pineapple
1 cup crushed canned peaches
1 pkg. chopped pecans
1 large pkg. cream cheese
1 large pkg. small marshmellows

¼ lb. white seedless grapes (halved)
¼ lb. fresh cherries
½ pint whipped cream
4 cups boiling water
4 cups ice water

Dissolve jello in boiling water. Add ice water. Place in refrigerator. When mixture congeals slightly, add fruit, marshmellows, cheese, and nuts. Mix well. Stir in whipped cream. Place in refrigerator until congealed. May be served with lettuce and mayonnaise as a salad or alone as a dessert.

Mrs. J. D. Roberts
Raleigh, North Carolina

FRUITED SOUR CREAM

8 peaches (pared and sliced)
1 cup brown sugar

2 cups sour cream

Combine sugar and sour cream. Alternate layers of peaches and sour cream in glass bowl. Serves 6.

Mrs. Frederick (Jane) Haynes, Jr.
Spartanburg

63

HEAVENLY HASH DESSERT

1 small can crushed pineapple
1 small bottle cherries
1 pint whipped cream

½ cup pecans
1 ripe banana

Combine ingredients and serve.

Mrs. Loring Ellis
Hampton

HOT FRUIT

1 medium can sliced pineapple
1 medium can peach halves
1 jar red apple rings
1 can pear halves
2 Tbs. flour

½ cup brown sugar
1 stick butter
1 cup sherry

Drain fruit. Cut fruit in half if large. Arrange fruit in 2 to 2½ quart casserole dish. Combine last four ingredients in top of double boiler until smooth and thickened. Pour over fruit. Cover and refrigerate overnight. Before serving, heat in oven at 350⁰ for 20 to 25 minutes or until bubbly. Serve in sherbert dishes with meat or over pound cake.

Mrs. Earle C. Traynham, Jr.
Columbia

Ice Cream

BANANA ICE CREAM

½ tsp. banana flavoring
1 can cream (Carnation) large
1½ qts. sweet milk
5 eggs

6 bananas (small)
2¼ cups sugar
25 lbs. ice
1 box ice cream salt

Bring eggs, milk and sugar to a boil. Cool slightly and add bananas and flavoring. Freeze in hand churn.

Mrs. Allen B. Thomas
Aiken

FRESH FIG ICE CREAM

1 pint light cream
1 pint whole milk
4 eggs, separated
¼ cup sweet cream sherry
¼ cup strained honey

1 cup sugar
4 cups Celeste figs, fresh
  picked and crushed
  after peeling
(Measure figs after peeling and
  before crushing)

Scald the cream and milk together. Add the sugar and honey, stir well. Beat the egg yolks until foamy and add to milk mixture. Beat the egg whites until very stiff. Mix the sherry with the crushed figs, then stir until well mixed with milk-egg yolk mixture. Fold in the stiffly beaten egg whites. Cool and turn into two ice trays and freeze. Beat up well when half frozen and return to freezer until firm. Serves 8 to 10.

Mrs. John C. (Eva) Key
Isle of Palms

PEANUT BUTTER ICE CREAM

1½ cups Graham cracker
  crumbs
¼ cup sugar
½ cup margarine (melted)

½ cup whipping cream
1 qt. vanilla ice cream
½ cup chunk-style
  peanut butter

Mix cracker crumbs, sugar, and margarine. Reserve 1 to 2 tablespoons of crumbs for garnish. Press remaining crumbs into 9 inch pie plate. Chill. Whip the cream. Place 1 quart of vanilla ice cream in mixing bowl. Stir just to soften. Fold in peanut butter. Then carefully fold in whipped cream. Quickly spoon ice cream mixture into chilled Graham cracker crust. Sprinkle reserved crumbs around edge to garnish pie. Freeze until firm. Remove from freezer 10 to 15 minutes before serving.

Ruth Ann Collins
Columbia

LEMON ICE CREAM

6 lemons　　　　　　　　3 cups heavy cream
3 eggs　　　　　　　　　2½ cups sugar
3 cups milk

Slice lemons thin, remove seeds and cover with 1 cup sugar. Scald milk over double boiler. Beat eggs and remaining sugar together, slowly add milk. Return to double boiler and cook, stirring constantly, until thick. Chill. Mix with cream, lemons, and juice. Freeze in electric freezer.

Mrs. Clement F. Haynsworth, Jr.
Greenville

MAE-MAE'S CUSTARD ICE CREAM

3 cups sugar　　　　　　10 eggs
½ tsp. salt　　　　　　　1 gallon milk
8 scant Tbs. flour　　　　Vanilla to taste

Combine sugar, salt and flour. Add beaten eggs. Set your pan of milk in another pan of water and heat the milk on top of the stove until the milk is scalding. Slowly add the egg mixture to the milk, stirring constantly. Continue to stir over low heat until the mixture is a custard-like consistency. Remove from heat and add vanilla. Store in the refrigerator until completely cooled. Freeze.

Mrs. David K. Summers, Sr.
Cameron

PLANTATION PINEAPPLE SHERBET

2 cups crushed, canned pineapple　　2 Tbs. lemon juice
1 cup sugar　　　　　　　　　　　1 tsp. plain gelatin
2 cups buttermilk　　　　　　　　　2 egg whites (beaten well)

In a tea cup, stir the gelatin into lemon juice. Combine the pineapple and the buttermilk, add the sugar. Set the lemon juice with gelatin in hot water, stir until completely dissolved and stir

66

into pineapple mixture. Fold in the beaten egg whites. Turn into an ice tray and and freeze, remove and beat once when freezing is taking place. Should freeze at least three hours. Serves 6. This sherbet is a fine summer dessert and tastes best if allowed to stand a few hours to mellow after freezing.

Mrs. John C. (Eva) Key
Isle of Palms

Pies

JODY'S FAVORITE APPLE PIE

6 or 7 apples (peeled,
  cored and sliced)
1 cup light brown sugar
  (firmly packed)
¼ tsp. nutmeg

Dash cinnamon
¼ tsp. salt
1 tsp. lemon juice
Rind ½ lemon (grated)
2 Tbs. butter

Line pie plate with pastry. Put apple slices in layers, sprinkling each layer with mixture of brown sugar, spices, salt, lemon juice, and lemon rind. Dot with butter and cover with top crust. Bake in hot oven. (450⁰) for 15 to 20 minutes, then reduce heat to 350⁰ for 20 to 30 minutes until crust is brown and apples tender.

Mrs. J. B. Traywick, II
Spartanburg

DATE-NUT PIE

4 egg whites (beaten stiff)
1 scant cup sugar
16 saltines (crushed)
1 tsp. baking powder

1 cup broken nuts
1 tsp. vanilla
1 cup dates (cut)

Put in buttered pie pans. Cook slowly. Top with whipped cream and add cherry with stem. Yields two pies.

Mrs. John Drummond
Ninety Six

CONCORD GRAPE PIE

4 cups grapes	¼ tsp. cinnamon
1 egg (beaten)	¼ tsp. cloves
1 cup light brown sugar	2 Tbs. butter
2 Tbs. flour	Pie pastry

Slip hulls from grapes and put the pulps in top of double boiler. Cook for 20 minutes. Steam hulls in separate pot until pastry is tender (add only enough water to keep them from sticking and cook over medium to low heat). Mash pulp through a sieve to remove the seeds and add pulp to the hulls. Cool. Beat the egg and add it. Sift the dry ingredients and combine with the grapes. Line a pie plate with pastry and sprinkle the crust with a small amount of flour. Add the grape mixture, dot with bits of butter, cover with top crust (whole or latticed) and bake for 10 minutes at 400^0 and then at 300^0 for 30 minutes. Lots of trouble, but I promise it's worth it. Serves 6.

Miss Lillian Watson
Mullins

GRASSHOPPER PIE

Pie Crust

24 hydrox chocolate cookies   4 tsp. melted butter (¼ cup)

Roll cookies very fine, add melted butter and blend. Use 9-inch pie plate. Chill in refrigerator while preparing the filling.

Filling

24 large marshmallows	2 oz. cream de menthe
2/3 cup hot milk	1 oz. cream de cocoa
½ pint whipping cream	

Dissolve marshmallows in hot milk. When dissolved set aside to cool. Whip cream until stiff. Fold in cream de menthe and cream de cocoa. Fold into cooled marshmallow mix. Pour into pie shell and grate chocolate shivers on top. Put in refrigerator overnight. Take out a few minutes before serving, so crust will not crack.

Mrs. W. Frank Partridge, Jr.
Newberry

PEACH PECAN PIE

1 cup sugar
3 Tbs. flour
2 Tbs. cornstarch
1 Tbs. orange juice
3 Tbs. butter

1 Tbs. grated orange peel
¼ cup chopped pecans
2 (or more) cups sliced
 peaches

Mix sugar, flour, and cornstarch. Add orange juice and butter. Cook over low heat until thick. Remove from heat. Add orange peel, nuts, and peaches. Pour into a 9 inch pastry-lined pie pan. Bake in 450^0 oven for 10 minutes. Then in 325^0 oven for 30 minutes.

Mrs. T. Dewey Wise
Mt. Pleasant

LIDDY'S EASY PINEAPPLE COCONUT PIES

1 stick margarine (melted)
2 cups sugar
1 cup chopped nuts
4 eggs

1 small can coconut
1 small can crushed pineapple
 (drained)

Beat eggs to thick foam. Add remaining ingredients and stir well. Put into 2 unbaked pastry shells and bake at 350^0 until golden brown. Makes 2 pies.

Mrs. Paul Murph
Whitestone

PINEAPPLE COCONUT PIE

4 eggs
1¼ cups sugar
1 small can crushed pineapple

1 cup Angel Flake coconut
1 stick oleo

Beat eggs well, add sugar, pineapple, and coconut. Melt oleo and add. Put in uncooked pie shell and bake at 325⁰ for 1 hour. Makes 2 pies.

Mrs. Belle Scott
Clinton

BLACK BOTTOM PIE

3 egg whites (beaten stiff)
¾ cup sugar
¾ cup Nabisco Famous Chocolate
   Wafers (crushed)

½ cup chopped pecans
1 tsp. vanilla
Whipped cream

Beat egg whites until stiff. Gradually add the ¾ cup sugar and beat again until real stiff. By hand fold in the crushed chocolate wafers, chopped nuts and vanilla. Place in 9 inch buttered pie pan. Bake 350⁰ for 25 to 30 minutes. Top with whipped cream.

Mrs. Earle C. Traynham, Jr.
Columbia

LOCH DHU CHOCOLATE PIE

4 squares chocolate
2 cups sugar
5 Tbs. cornstarch
2 Tbs. butter

1 tsp. vanilla
2½ cups milk
6 egg yolks (beaten)
½ tsp. salt

Melt chocolate. Scald milk, add sugar, butter, and cornstarch mixed with the ½ cup cold milk. Cook, stirring all the time in a double boiler. When it begins to thicken, add the chocolate, the beaten egg yolks, and the salt. Thoroughly beat with egg beater and cook until mixture thickens. Beat again, adding the vanilla. Pour into cooked deep crust. Pile high with meringue made from egg whites beaten stiff and 7 tablespoons of sugar. Bake at 300⁰ for 45 minutes. Serve cold, but do not put the pie in the refrigerator. Yields 2 shallow pies or 1 deep one.

Elizabeth Gaillard Simons
Loch Dhu Plantation
Eutawville

FUDGE PIE

½ cup Crisco
1 cup sugar
2 eggs
2 or 3 squares chocolate

1/3 cup flour
1 tsp. vanilla
¾ cup pecans

Cream sugar and shortening, then add well beaten eggs. Melt chocolate and add to this. Blend in flour and vanilla and when mixed add nutmeats. Bake in well-greased round pie or cake pan at 325⁰ for 30 minutes. Let cool slightly in pan, before removing to plate. Cut into 6 or 8 wedges and serve with whipped cream or ice cream topping.

Mrs. Heyward S. Singley
Columbia

FRENCH SILK CHOCOLATE PIE

When I grew up, my favorite pastime was to fix this recipe for French Silk Chocolate Pie which was my mother's. It is a great dessert for company dinners.

1½ sticks butter or oleo
1½ oz. bitter chocolate
¾ cup sugar

2 eggs (unbeaten)
1 tsp. vanilla

Use electric mixer, medium speed. Cream butter, add sugar gradually, creaming mixture thoroughly. Blend in chocolate (melted and cooled). Add vanilla. Add eggs, one at a time, beating 5 minutes after each addition. Pour into 8 inch pie shell. Chill. Top with whipped cream.

Mrs. Strom Thurmond
Aiken

FUDGE CHESS PIE

1½ cups sugar
3 Tbs. cocoa
2 well-beaten eggs

1 tsp. vanilla
½ stick butter
2/3 cup half & half

Mix. Bake at 325⁰ in unbaked 10-inch pie shell (or 2 smaller pie shells). Serve with whipped cream.

Mary Anne Crocker
Alexandria, Virginia

LEMON FILLING

1 Tbs. butter
2 Tbs. flour
1 cup sugar

1 egg
½ cup water
Juice and rind of 2 lemons

Blend butter and flour. Add sugar, water, egg and lemon. Mix well. Cook in double boiler until thickened (about 20 minutes).

Mrs. J. W. Hunt
Pittsboro, North Carolina

LEMON MERINGUE PIE

1 (9 in.) pastry shell
¼ cup cornstarch
2 Tbs. flour
1 cup sugar
¼ tsp. salt
2 cups boiling water

3 eggs (separated)
2 Tbs. butter
1 Tbs. grated lemon peel
6 Tbs. lemon juice
6 Tbs. sugar

Prepare baked pastry shell. Combine the cornstarch, flour, sugar, and salt in the top of a double boiler. Stir in boiling water. Gradually stir slightly beaten egg yolks into cornstarch mixture. Cook about 10 minutes, stirring frequently. Remove from heat. Stir in butter, lemon peel and juice. Cover and cool. Pour into pastry shell. Beat egg whites, gradually adding the 6 tablespoons sugar, until stiff peaks form. Spread meringue over lemon filling. Bake 3 to 5 minutes or until lightly browned.

Mrs. J. B. Traywick, II
Spartanburg

72

LEMON ANGEL PIE

4 egg whites
¼ tsp. cream of tartar
1 cup sugar
4 egg yolks
½ cup sugar

2 Tbs. grated lemon peel
¼ cup lemon juice
1 cup heavy cream

Heat oven to 275⁰. Grease 9 inch pie plate. Beat egg whites and cream of tartar until foamy. Beat in 1 cup sugar, 1 tablespoon at a time; this should take approximately 25 minutes. Spread meringue over bottom and sides of prepared pie plate; shape with back of spoon so bottom is ¼ inch thick and sides are 1 inch thick. Bake 60 minutes. Turn off oven; leave meringue shell in oven to cool 1 hour. Remove from oven. Cool to room temperature. Beat egg yolks in top of double boiler until thick and lemon colored. Beat in ½ cup sugar gradually. Blend in lemon peel and juice. Cook over hot, not boiling, water, stirring constantly five to eight minutes or until thick. Cool. Whip ¾ cup heavy cream until soft peaks form. Fold into lemon mixture. Turn into cooled meringue shell. Chill at least four hours. Before serving, whip remaining cream; spoon onto center of pie. Makes 8 servings.

Mrs. Bill Jordan
Greenville

PECAN PIE

4 eggs
1 cup sugar
1 cup light corn syrup
½ Tbs. flour
¼ tsp. salt

1 tsp. vanilla extract
¼ cup butter (melted)
2 cups pecan halves
Whipped cream (if desired)
9 inch unbaked pie shell

Prepare the pie shell and refrigerate. Preheat oven to 350⁰. To make filling—in medium bowl, with rotary beater, beat eggs well. Add the sugar, corn syrup, flour, salt, and vanilla. Beat well. Stir in butter and pecans until well combined. Pour mixture into unbaked pie shell. Bake 60 minutes or until filling is set in the center. Cool pie completely on a wire rack. Chill slightly before serving.

Catha W. Reid
West Columbia

DRUMMOND'S PECAN PIE

4 egg yolks
2 cups sugar
2 cups sour cream
½ cup flour (sifted)

½ tsp. lemon extract
¼ tsp. salt
2 unbaked pie shells

Topping

4 egg whites
2 cups brown sugar

2 cups broken pecan
    meats

Mix egg yolks, sugar, sour cream, flour, lemon extract, and salt. Cook the mixture over water until thickened, or about 45 minutes. Spoon the mixture into 2 unbaked pie shells. For the topping, beat the egg whites and brown sugar. Stir in pecan meats. Then spread over pie filling and bake in a 325⁰ oven until brown, or about 15 minutes. Makes two 9 inch pies.

Mrs. John Drummond
Ninety Six

DERBY PIE

¾ stick melted butter
¾ cup white sugar
¾ cup white corn syrup
3 eggs

1 tsp. vanilla
¾ cup chopped pecans
    or hickory nuts
½ cup chocolate chips

Cream butter and sugar together. Mix in syrup, eggs, vanilla. Stir in pecans and chocolate chips and pour into unbaked pie shell. Bake in 350⁰ oven for 45 minutes to one hour. Serve slightly warm with a big dollop of whipped cream on each slice.

Mrs. John C. West
Governor's Mansion
Columbia

BUTTERMILK COCONUT PIE

¼ stick margarine   1 can coconut
1 cup plus 2 Tbs. sugar   2 eggs
¼ cup buttermilk

Cream together the margarine and sugar. Add eggs and buttermilk until blended. Add coconut last. Pour into uncooked pie shell and bake about 1 hour at 350⁰.

Mrs. E. L. Bolick
Central

EASY FROZEN PIE

1 pkg. chocolate chip macaroons   Milk
1 large bowl Cool Whip

Line a pie plate with macaroons which have been dipped very quickly into milk. Spoon Cool Whip over cookies, then add another layer of milk-dipped macaroons and a final layer of Cool Whip. Freeze. Serve frozen.

Mrs. J. B. Traywick, II
Spartanburg

CREAM CHEESE PIE CRUST

1 stick butter   1 cup flour
3 oz. cream cheese

Cream butter with cream cheese and add flour. Pie crust will be soft pad in pan. Excellent for pecan pie or chicken pie.

Mrs. Richard (Betty) Boykin
Hampton, Virginia

75

Miscellaneous

ONE POT BROWNIES

2 (2 oz.) squares unsweetened
  chocolate
1/3 cup shortening
1 cup sugar
2 eggs

¾ cup flour
½ tsp. salt
½ tsp. baking powder
½ cup chopped nuts.

Heat oven to 350⁰. Melt chocolate and shortening together in pot. Let cool, then beat in sugar and eggs. Sift flour, baking powder and salt together; stir in. Add nuts. Bake 25 to 30 minutes.

Chocolate Icing

Melt one square chocolate and 1 tablespoon butter together. Beat in a cup confectioners' sugar and milk until it is of spreading consistency. Spread on brownies while still warm.

Mrs. Hazel Martin
West Columbia

CHOCOLATE BROWNIES

2 sticks margarine
4 squares baking chocolate
2 cups sugar
4 eggs
1 1/3 cups plain flour

1 tsp. baking powder
½ tsp. salt
1 cup chopped pecans
2 tsp. vanilla

Melt margarine and chocolate together. Beat eggs. Mix in sugar. Add the chocolate mixture. Then, add flour, baking powder, salt, which have been sifted together. Mix in the vanilla and nuts. Spread on lightly greased bottom of two shallow pans. (9x9x11 inches or one large baking pan). Bake in 350⁰ oven for 25 minutes or until just done. Do not over-bake. Cut into squares while hot. Recipe yields four dozen brownies.

Mrs. R. L. Reid
Charlotte, North Carolina

BROWNIES FOR A CROWD

2 cups sugar (brown or white)
1 cup margarine
4 eggs
5 Tbs. cocoa

4 Tbs. milk
2 cups flour
2 tsp. vanilla

Mix sugar, margarine and eggs for 2 minutes. Add remaining ingredients and mix well. Turn into a greased pan (10 x 15 inches) that has been dusted with cocoa. Bake in 350⁰ oven for 15 minutes.

Mrs. Odd Thorsen
Rock Hill

SAUCEPAN BROWNIES

1 stick margarine
2 (1 oz.) squares semi-sweet chocolate
¾ cup sugar
1 cup nuts (if desired)

1 cup flour
1 tsp. baking powder
1 tsp. vanilla
2 eggs (slightly beaten)

Melt butter and chocolate in a saucepan. Remove from heat and add all ingredients except eggs. Mix well and add slightly beaten eggs. Pour into a greased 9 inch pan and bake at 350⁰ for 30 minutes.

Mrs. J. W. Waddill
Columbia

COCONUT CONES

1 lb. powdered sugar
½ lb. fresh grated coconut

5 egg whites

Whip eggs as for frosting, adding sugar while beating until frosting stands alone. Beat in coconut. Mold mixture into small cones. Place on waxed paper. Bake in very moderate oven until lightly browned.

Ann M. Aycock
Jonesville

77

COCONUT PUFFS

3 egg whites
1 cup confectioners' sugar
1 Tbs. cornstarch

2 cups coconut
1 tsp. vanilla

Beat egg whites until stiff, add sugar, stir over steam until sticks. Remove from steam, add cornstarch, coconut, vanilla. Drop from spoon on buttered tin, dust with flour. Bake in slow oven.

Mrs. Doris Herring
Columbia

SLICED DATE ROLL

1 lb. pitted dates
(finely ground)
3 or 4 pieces candied
ginger (finely chopped)

Sugar
2/3 cup coarsely chopped
pecans or English walnuts

Mix dates, ginger, and nuts. Knead on board sprinkled with sugar. Make into rolls, wrap in wax paper. Refrigerate. Slice before serving.

Ann M. Aycock
Jonesville

DELTA BARS

½ cup soft shortening
1 cup sugar
1 whole egg
1 egg yolk
1 tsp. vanilla or lemon flavoring
1½ cups sifted plain flour

1 tsp. baking powder
½ tsp. salt

Mix all ingredients thoroughly. Spread in greased pan (13 x 9 x 2 inches).

78

Topping

1 egg white

1 cup light brown sugar

½ cup nuts (finely chopped)

Beat egg white until foamy. Add gradually brown sugar and beat until stiff. Fold in nuts. Spread over dough in pan. Bake 25 minutes at 375⁰. Cut while warm into 24 squares.

Miss Lillian Watson
Mullins

GINGERBREAD

2 cups flour
2 tsp. baking powder
2 tsp. ginger
1 tsp. cinnamon
½ tsp. salt

1/3 cup butter
½ cup sugar
1 egg
2/3 cup molasses
¾ cup milk

Heat oven to 350⁰. Grease and flour pan. Sift dry ingredients together. Mix with butter, milk, molasses and egg. Beat until smooth. Pour into pan. Bake at 350⁰ for 45 to 50 minutes. Serve with lemon sauce while still warm.

Mrs. Hazel Martin
West Columbia

MRS. CROUCH'S LEMON-PECAN WHIRL

1 cup sugar
3 eggs
1 stick butter
1 box lemon "jello"

1 can crushed pineapple
1 lb. vanilla wafers
1 cup ground pecans

Cream egg yolks, sugar, and butter. Add jello which has been dissolved in ¾ cup of hot water. Add one cup of nuts and one-cup of vanilla wafers. Add pineapple and last of all fold in egg whites. Put ½ of crumbs on bottom of pan and the remainder on top. Refrigerate and serve with whipped cream.

Mrs. T. Dewey Wise
Mt. Pleasant

LEMON FROSTED COCONUT BARS

½ cup butter or margarine
1½ cups brown sugar
1¼ cups plain flour (sifted)
2 eggs (beaten)
1 tsp. baking powder

1 tsp. vanilla extract
½ tsp. salt
1 cup flaked coconut
¾ cup finely chopped
  blanched almonds

Preheat oven to 350⁰. Cream butter and brown sugar until light. Add flour and mix well. Press mixture evenly into bottom of a 13x9x2 inch baking pan. Bake about 10 to 15 minutes. Beat eggs, vanilla, and remaining 1 cup brown sugar until frothy. Sift together remaining ¼ cup flour, baking powder, and salt. Fold into egg mixture. Add coconut, almonds, and mix well. Spread evenly over first mixture, which had cooled. Bake for about 20 minutes. Cool in pan.

Frosting

2 cups confectioners' sugar
  (sifted)
¼ cup half and half cream

1 lemon rind (grated)
2 tsp. lemon juice

Mix and stir in double boiler over just simmering water until smooth and shiny. Cool a little, then pour over coconut mixture. When cold, cut into 24 bars.

Mrs. Lawrence R. Dixon, III
Florence

TOASTED SNOW SQUARES

1 envelope unflavored gelatin
4 Tbs. cold water
1 cup boiling water
2/3 cup sugar
3 egg whites (unbeaten)

¼ tsp. salt
1 tsp. vanilla
16 graham crackers
  (rolled fine)

80

Sprinkle gelatin over cold water and let soak for five minutes. Add boiling water and stir until dissolved. Let cool slightly. Add egg whites, salt, and vanilla. Beat with rotary mixer until mixture is light and resembles thick cream. Turn into a 9x9x2 inch pan. Chill. Cut into squares. Roll in graham cracker crumbs. Arrange in serving glasses. Top with butter sauce.

Butter Sauce

2 egg yolks	1 Tbs. grated lemon rind
1/3 cup sugar	2 Tbs. lemon juice
1/3 cup melted butter	1/3 cup heavy cream (whipped)

Beat egg yolks until thick and lemon-colored. Gradually add sugar and continue to beat. Add butter, lemon rind, and lemon juice. Blend. Fold in cream. Chill.

Mrs. Holly B. Smoak
Meggett

PETTICOAT TAILS

This is a third generation recipe, brought from France to Scotland by Mary, Queen of Scots. The French name, "Petits Gateaux Tailles," means "little cakes cut off." But the name came to be pronounced as it sounded to the Scotch and English—"Petticoat Tails."

1 cup soft butter	¼ tsp. salt
1 cup confectioners' sugar	2½ flour (sifted)
1 tsp. sherry (or other flavoring)	Pecan halves or crystallized cherries

Combine butter, sugar, sherry, salt, and flour. Mix thoroughly with hands. Press and mold into rolls about 1½ in diameter. Wrap in wax paper, chill until firm. Slice, place pecan or cherry on each cookie. Place on cookie sheet. Bake at 350⁰ until lightly browned.

Mrs. S. Gordon Brown
Cheraw

Meats

BEEF BOURGUIGNONNE

4 lbs. lean beef (cut
  in cubes)
1 tsp. Monosodium glutamate
1½ tsp. salt
¼ tsp. pepper
½ cup butter
2/3 cup diced carrot
2 cups diced onion
¼ cup flour
2 cloves garlic (sliced)
1/8 tsp. thyme
2 bay leaves
½ cup chopped parsley
1½ cups dry red wine
  (Burgundy, preferable)

2 cups beef bouillon (2 cans
  Campbell beef bouillon)
20 small carrots (small
  carrot nuggets, frozen
  in butter)
20 tiny white onions
  (canned, drained)
½ lb. small fresh mushrooms
  (B&B brand, in butter)
¼ cup brandy (optional)

Sprinkle beef cubes with Monosodium glutamate, salt and pepper. Allow to stand few minutes. Melt half of butter in Dutch oven. Add beef cubes and brown. Add diced vegetables. Mix in flour, garlic, thyme, bay leaf and ¼ cup parsley. Add wine and bouillon. Stir well. (Cover meat with liquid.) Cover and simmer 1½ hours or until almost tender. Brown whole onions and carrots in remaining ¼ cup butter. Remove from pan and sauté mushrooms. Add carrots and onions to meat and cook covered 30 minutes. Add mushrooms and cook 15 minutes longer. Sprinkle with remaining parsley. Serve with rice or noodles.

Mrs. Thomas T. Traywick, Sr.
Cope

BEEF BURGUNDY

1½ lbs. round steak
Flour
Salt and pepper
Cooking oil
1 onion (chopped)
1 cup burgundy wine

1 can sliced mushrooms
1 bay leaf
2 cups water
Instant parsley
Powdered garlic

Cut steak into large cubes and shake well in a bag with flour, salt and pepper. Brown in oil along with onion. Add about 2 cups water and 1 bay leaf. Steam for 1 hour. Then add mushrooms, pinch of parsley, pinch of garlic, and a cup of burgundy wine. Simmer until mushrooms are tender and remove bay leaf. Serve over hot rice. Serves 6.

Mrs. Rose Wilkins
Lexington

ROPA VIEJA

1 (12 oz.) can of roast beef
2 Tbs. of olive oil
3 cloves of garlic (chopped
  fine)
4 large onions (diced)
2 or 3 stalks celery with
  leaves (chopped very fine)
1 (10 oz.) can of tomatoes

1 large green pepper
  (cut coarsely)
2 Tbs. Worcestershire sauce
3 dashes of seasoned salt
1 (2 oz.) bottle olives
  (sliced)
Lots of freshly ground
  pepper

Shred the beef, tearing it into stringy pieces. Remove any of the fat from the meat. Place the oil in frying pan and heat. Add the onion, garlic and celery and cook slowly until its soft. Add juice and about half the tomato from the can. Simmer about 15 minutes, add the meat and mix well. Add the green pepper, Worcestershire, seasoned salt and black pepper. Cover and simmer over low heat for about 3 hours. After that time all the liquid should be absorbed into the meat. About 10 minutes before serving add the olives. Serve with grits with butter and cheese or over rice. Makes 2 to 3 servings.

Mrs. Tom W. Elliott
Columbia

BEEF ROLL CORDON BLEU

1 pkg. saltines (20)	1 tsp. salt
1½ lbs. ground round steak	Dash pepper
2 eggs (beaten)	5 slices ham
¼ cup milk	(thinly sliced)
1 Tbs. minced onion	8 oz. Swiss cheese (sliced)

Crumble saltines and combine with meat, eggs, milk, salt, and pepper. Mix lightly, but thoroughly. Place on waxed paper. Moisten with water and make into rectangle (½x14x10 inches). Arrange ham and cheese over meat. Roll meat, as jelly roll. Shape into compact roll. Seal ends and seam very securely. Place seam side down and chill at least 3 hours (or better, overnight). Bake at 350⁰ for 1½ hours. Remove from oven and let stand for 10 minutes. Slice and serve with basic white sauce to which Swiss cheese from package has been added. Serves 6 to 8.

J. Kirkland Grant
Columbia

COUNTRY STYLE STEAK

This recipe has been a traditional "family-night supper" favorite at Fishing Creek Presbyterian Church in Chester County since 1752.

Steak	Cooking Oil
Salt	2-3 Tbs. cornstarch (sifted)

Cut steak into medium size pieces and salt each piece. Brown thoroughly in large frying pan with a medium amount of cooking oil. After steaks are nicely browned, set the grease aside for future use in making gravy. Remove all portions of browned steaks and place in a pressure cooker, adding enough water to more than cover steak. (If you have a rack, it is advisable that it be placed in the bottom of the pressure cooker before putting in steaks and water.) Cool steak in pressure cooker for 20 minutes or more, or until tender.

Miss Mary Ann Armstrong
Chester

PEPPER STEAK

1/3 cup salad oil or lard
1 tsp. salt
Pepper to taste
1½ lb. lean beef
6 Tbs. minced onions
1 clove garlic (chopped fine)

4 green peppers (finely diced)
1½ cups celery
1½ cups beef bouillon
2 Tbs. cornstarch
¼ cup water
3 tsp. Soy sauce

In a preheated, heavy, 10-inch skillet heat salad oil or lard, salt and a little pepper to taste. Cut lean beef (tenderloin, top round or sirloin) across the grain into strips ¼ inch wide and 1½ inches long. Brown the strips in hot oil over a high flame, stirring constantly. Add minced onions or scallions, garlic, celery sliced diagonally into ¼-inch pieces, and cook, stirring for a few minutes longer. Add beef bouillon, cover the pan tightly and cook over a moderate flame about 10 minutes, until the meat and vegetables are tender. Add cornstarch mixed to a paste with water and Soy sauce. Cook for a few minutes more, stirring constantly, until the liquid thickens and the mixture is very hot. Serve immediately with fluffy white rice.

Mrs. Hal Kirven
Darlington

MEAT PIE

1 lb. ground sirloin
4 large potatoes (mashed)
Bisquick

1 onion (chopped)
Salt and pepper to taste

Barely cover meat with water. Add more water gradually while cooking. Boil ground sirloin until done. Add chopped onion and salt and pepper to taste. Boil at medium heat. Mash the potatoes. Mix dough and roll out on cutting board. Cover bottom of medium size casserole dish with thinly rolled dough. Bake until almost done. Add ground sirloin. Smooth potatoes on top. Cover casserole with remaining dough. Press edges tightly. Bake in oven at 350⁰ for about 45 minutes.

Mrs. Earle Morris
Columbia

BEEF STROGANOFF

1½ lbs. ground beef
1 tsp. salt
¼ tsp. pepper
1 clove garlic (chopped)
¼ cup bread crumbs
1 egg
¼ cup water
3 Tbs. oil or fat

1 large onion (sliced)
1 cup mushrooms (sliced)
2 cups canned beef bouillon
3 Tbs. sherry
2 Tbs. flour
2 Tbs. tomato sauce
1 tsp. dry mustard
2/3 cup sour cream

Combine beef, salt, pepper, garlic, bread crumbs, egg, and water. Shape into 24 or more medium sized meat balls. Heat 2 tablespoons of fat. Sauté mushrooms and onions about 15 minutes until brown. Remove to dish. Add remaining fat to fry pan. When sizzling, drop in meat balls a few at a time and brown on all sides. Meat should remain rare inside. Drain. Add to dish with mushrooms and onions. Add flour to fry pan and brown well. Add beef bouillon, slowly stirring to make a smooth paste. Add sherry, tomato paste (or sauce), and mustard. Blend well. Add meat, mushrooms, and onions. Simmer for 15 minutes. Five minutes before serving, add sour cream and blend well into sauce.

Mr. & Mrs. R. D. Coble
Pensacola, Florida

GROUND BEEF SKILLET CASSEROLE

1 lb. ground beef
Salt and pepper to taste
1 cup chopped green peppers
1 cup chopped celery

1 cup chopped onions
1 cup uncooked rice
1 can tomatoes
1½ cans water

Brown beef in heavy skillet and add salt and pepper. Add other ingredients, in the order listed, separately. Cook over high flame for 10 minutes. Remove from heat, cover and set aside for at least one hour.

Mrs. Rachel Montgomery
Camden

87

HER HONOR'S SPECIAL CASSEROLE

1 lb. lean, ground chuck
1 medium green pepper, chopped
1 medium onion, chopped
1 can tomatoes (1 lb. size)
1 can whole kernel corn
  (1 lb. size)
1 tsp. salt

Pepper to taste
1 Tbs. Worcestershire sauce
1½ cups grated, sharp
  cheddar cheese
1 package thinly sliced
  noodles (8 oz. size)

Brown the meat, onion and green pepper over low heat in heavy iron skillet with two tablespoons of shortening. Add tomatoes, corn and seasoning, simmer 20 minutes, add noodles and ½ cup water. Cook until noodles begin to get tender. Turn into a buttered casserole, top with grated cheese and bake at 325⁰ for 45 minutes. Serves 8.

Mrs. John C. (Eva) Key
Mt. Pleasant

STUFFED BELL PEPPERS

6 medium bell peppers
6 slices bacon (fried
  crisp)
1 onion (chopped)
3 stalks celery (chopped)
5 slices bread
1 (no. 1) can sardines

4 eggs
2 Tbs. bacon drippings
3 Tbs. Worcestershire sauce
3 Tbs. catsup
3 Tbs. mustard
1 Tbs. pepper
Salt to taste

Split bell peppers long way and remove seeds. Grease with bacon drippings. Combine bacon, onion, celery, bread, sardines, eggs. Add Worcestershire sauce, catsup, mustard, pepper, and salt if needed. Mix well. Place peppers on greased baking dish. Fill with mixture and bake at 450⁰ until brown on top.

Mrs. D. P. Wise
Orangeburg

BEEF STEW

2 lbs. beef stew meat
2 Tbs. fat
4 cups boiling water
1 tsp. lemon juice
1 tsp. Worcestershire sauce
1 clove garlic
1 medium onion (sliced)
2 bay leaves

1 Tbs. salt
½ tsp. black pepper
½ tsp. paprika
Dash of allspice or cloves
1 tsp. sugar
6 carrots
4 small potatoes

Thoroughly brown meat in hot fat, using a large 3 or 4 quart pan. Add water, lemon juice, Worcestershire sauce, garlic, sliced onion, bay leaves, and seasonings. Simmer 2 hours, stirring occasionally. Add carrots and potatoes. Cook until vegetables are done (about 20 minutes). Thicken liquid for gravy if desired.

Mrs. J. B. Traywick, II
Spartanburg

SUNDAY STEW

1 lb. boneless beef stew
1 can onion soup
1 can mushroom soup
2 white potatoes (cut
  into eighths)

2 carrots (cut into
  eighths)
2 Tbs. sherry

Mix all ingredients except sherry. Bake in casserole at 300⁰ for 3 hours. Add sherry and serve over rice.

Mrs. Ann M. McDonald
Sumter

HOT DOG CHILI

1 lb. pork sausage
1 small onion (chopped)
1 Tbs. chili powder

1 Tbs. mustard
3 Tbs. catsup
1 cup water

Brown sausage in frypan. Add remaining ingredients. Cover and cook for 30 minutes.

Mrs. Thyra S. Robinson
Lake Placid, Florida

SLOPPY JOES FOR FIFTY PEOPLE

10 lbs. hamburger
2 cups onion (chopped)
1/3 cup salt
2 tsp. pepper
1 Tbs. chili powder

1 Tbs. sugar
1 Tbs. vinegar
½ cup prepared mustard
1 pint catsup
¼ cup Worcestershire sauce

Brown hamburger and onion. Add other ingredients and simmer for 1½ hours.

Mrs. Odd Thorsen
Rock Hill

CAROLINA CHILI

8-10 slices breakfast bacon
6 onions (chopped)
2 lbs. lean ground beef
2 (No. 2) cans tomatoes
2 (small) cans tomato sauce

2 tsp. salt
1 Tbs. black pepper
Chili powder
2 (No. 2) cans red
   kidney beans

Fry bacon until crisp, remove and reserve for final mixture. In bacon grease, fry onions until soft and remove. Crumble ground beef into same bacon grease, cook until gray. In large saucepan, combine ground beef, onions, tomatoes, tomato sauce, salt, pepper, chili powder (add to taste). Cook slowly for 1 hour or slightly more, stirring frequently. Add beans, continue to simmer. Just before serving, add crumbled crisp bacon and stir into mixture. Serve hot, over rice or in bowls. A bit of garlic cooked with onions improves flavor.

Miss Mary Henderson
Augusta, Georgia

CHILI

2 cans (1 lb.) tomatoes
(mashed)
2 cans (15 oz.) red kidney
beans
1½ lb. hamburger meat
2 large onions (chopped fine)
1 large bell pepper

¼ tsp. red pepper
(optional)
2 Tbs. cooking oil
½ cup water
2 Tbs. Sugar
2 Tbs. chili powder
2 Tbs. flour

Salt and pepper hamburger meat. Form meat into small balls. Heat oil in large pot. Cook onions and pepper for 5 minutes. Cook onions until turn white, not brown. Add meat balls and cook until gray (about 10 minutes). Add tomatoes, water, and sugar. Mix in beans well. Cover and cook on low heat for 15 to 20 minutes. Mix chili powder with flour, adding enough water to make a thin paste. Add paste to pot gradually. Cook on low heat for 15 minutes. Serves 6.

Mrs. Allen B. Thomas, Jr.
Aiken

CHILI

3 lbs. lean ground beef
3 cans whole tomatoes
3 cans red kidney beans
(drained)

2 medium onions (chopped)
2 cans tomato sauce
1 can (tomato sauce)
water
Salt, pepper, chili powder

Brown ground beef and onions. Drain excess grease and put mixture in large dutch oven. Add tomatoes which have been broken into small pieces. Add tomato sauce and one sauce can of water. Stir in kidney beans. Add salt, pepper, and chili powder to taste. Cover and cook over low heat for 1 to 2 hours. It may be necessary to add water, depending on personal preference of thickness.

Bobbi Fraser
Simpsonville

91

TACOS

1 can (11 oz., 18 count)
  tortillas
6 Tbs. grease (Crisco)
1 lb. ground chuck
2 small tomatoes (diced)

¼ head lettuce (shredded)
Salt
Pepper
Tabasco sauce

In fry pan, heat grease to 350⁰, soften tortillas in grease until they bend, raise heat to 375⁰, cook folded tortillas until crisp. Drain on paper towels, keep warm in a 250⁰ oven for 10 minutes before serving. Cook ground chuck in fry pan, scrambling into small pieces. Salt and pepper to taste. Mix with tomatoes and lettuce, stuff each fried tortilla as a sandwich. Serve hot with Tabasco sauce.

Mrs. Carrie Jerome Anderson
Rock Hill

Mrs. G. H. Simpson
Lexington, Virginia

SPICY MEXICAN CASSEROLE

1 (10 oz.) can chili
¾ cup sour cream
½ cup hot peppers (use hot
  taco sauce or jalapeno
  pepper sauce)

1 medium can Mexicorn
  (drained)
Corn chips
Grated cheese

Arrange ingredients in layers in a casserole dish, starting with the chili and ending with the corn chips and cheese. Allow enough corn chips and cheese to cover the top of the dish. Place in a preheated 350⁰ oven for about 30 minutes until well heated and the cheese melts. Remove and serve hot. Serves 6.

Mary Brigman
Conway

SPAGHETTI WITH MEAT BALLS

Tomato Meat Sauce

¼ cup olive oil
½ cup onions (chopped)
½ lb. beef chuck
½ lb. pork shoulder
7 cups (2 No. 2½ cans)
  tomatoes

1 Tbs. salt
1 bay leaf
¾ cup (6 oz. can)
  tomato paste
½ cup water

Heat olive oil in large saucepan. Add onion, beef, and pork. Cook until lightly browned. Add mixture of tomatoes, salt, and bay leaf. Cover, simmer over very low heat for 2½ hours. Add tomato paste, simmer over low heat for 2 hours or until thickened. If too thick, add water. Remove meat and bay leaf from sauce.

Meat Balls

½ lb. ground beef
½ lb. ground pork
1 cup soft bread crumbs
1 Tbs. Parmesan cheese
 (grated)
1 Tbs. parsley (minced)

1 egg (well beaten)
1 tsp. salt
¼ tsp. pepper
2 Tbs. olive oil
1 clove garlic (minced)

Mix all but last two ingredients, shape into balls about 1 inch in diameter. Heat olive oil and garlic in skillet. Add meat balls, brown. Pour off fat. Add meat balls to tomato meat sauce about 20 minutes before sauce is done.

Spaghetti

4 qts. water
1 Tbs. salt

8 oz. spaghetti
(broken in half)

Boil rapidly uncovered for 10 to 12 minutes, or until spaghetti is tender. Drain in colander. Serve sauce and meat balls over spaghetti. Top with Parmesan or Romano cheese. Serves 4 to 6.

Mrs. Allen B. Thomas
Aiken

SUCCULENT SPAGHETTI

1 (8 oz.) pkg. fine spaghetti
6 slices bacon
1 onion (chopped fine)
1 lb. lean ground beef

2 (no. 2) cans tomatoes
2 cans tomato soup
1 can tomato juice
1 small can sliced
  mushrooms (optional)

Chop bacon into small pieces, fry. When almost done, add chopped onions, cook until soft and yellow, drain fat, add crumbled raw beef, and cook until done. Add mushrooms, tomato soup, and tomatoes. Add spaghetti that has been cooked by directions on package and drained. Stir. Pour tomato juice over all. Cook in 300⁰ oven for 1 hour. Stir occasionally. Serves 8.

Mrs. James M. Graham
Hartsville

CHEESE AND BACON HOT DOGS

1 pkg. all beef hot dogs
Cheddar cheese

5 strips bacon (raw)

Slit hot dogs lengthwise, pressing down to spread apart. Add 1 slice of cheese (about ¼ inch thick) and ½ strip of bacon to each hot dog. Place on cookie sheet and bake at 325⁰ until cheese and bacon starts bubbling, (about 15 minutes).

Agnes Nelson
Columbia

Chicken

BIRD OF PARADISE

4 boned chicken breasts (whole)
1 tsp. salt
1 stick butter
3 eggs

3 tsp. milk
1 cup cooking sherry
½ cup grated Parmesan cheese

94

Sprinkle salt over chicken. Melt butter in electric skillet at 300⁰. Beat eggs and milk. Dip chicken in egg mixture then roll in grated cheese. Brown on both sides then turn temperature to 225⁰ and add sherry. Cook covered for 45 minutes or until tender. Baste frequently while cooking. Serve with wild or herbed rice and serve with pan gravy.

Harry D. Smith
Atlanta, Georgia

CHICKEN DIVAN

2 tsp. salt
Few grains pepper
1 tsp. celery seed
1 medium onion (chopped)
1 garlic clove (crushed)
2 cups water

2 (10 oz.) pkgs. frozen
  broccoli spears
¼ cup milk
3 Tbs. dry sherry
1 tsp. Worcestershire
  sauce

Add first 5 ingredients to water in large saucepan. Add chicken breasts; simmer until tender. Let cool in broth. Remove skin; bone chicken and cut meat into bite-size pieces; set aside. Measure ½ cup broth; set aside. Cook broccoli in remaining broth. Combine milk, reserved broth, sherry and Worcestershire sauce in saucepan. Blend flour to thin paste with a little of this milk mixture; return to saucepan. Add ¾ of the grated cheese; stir over low heat until thick and smooth. Grease large, shallow casserole dish; arrange broccoli in a circle on bottom. Scatter chicken between and on top of broccoli spears. Top with mushroom slices; pour cheese sauce over all. Sprinkle with rest of cheese. Bake at 350⁰ for about 20 minutes. Serves six.

Sauce

1 Tbs. flour
2 Tbs. seasoned bread crumbs

10 oz. sharp cheddar cheese
  (grated)
1 (6 oz.) can sliced broiled
  mushrooms

Mr. & Mrs. R. D. Coble
Pensacola, Florida

95

CHICKEN FILLED CREPES

Filling

1 (3½ lb.) chicken	2½ cups reduced chicken stock
1 onion (chopped finely)	4 Tbs. grated Parmesan cheese
1 carrot (chopped roughly)	Spices:
2 cups chopped celery	salt
½ cup butter or margarine	white pepper
1 cup plain flour	nutmeg
2½ cups milk	cayenne pepper
½ cup dry white wine	parsley

Crepes

1 cup plain flour	Salt
1 whole egg plus 1 egg yolk	1 Tbs. butter
1¼ cups milk	

Make crepes batter by placing flour into a bowl, make a well in the center and add the egg, the egg yolk, and a dash of salt. Combine slowly with milk to form a smooth batter. Allow to stand 4 hours in the refrigerator. Melt some butter in a large (4½-5 quart) pan. Sauté carrot and onion for about 5 minutes. Add chicken and allow to steam for 5 more minutes. Cover chicken with cold water and bring to a simmer for 1¼ hours. Remove chicken and cut into small pieces. Reduce chicken stock to about 2½ cups by boiling rapidly. Strain chicken stock and discard carrots and onions.

To make crepes, melt one tablespoon of butter in a crepe pan or teflon frying pan. Add melted butter to crepes batter. Place a small portion (about ¼ cup) of the batter into the pan and roll it around so that it covers the pan base. Cook until waxy bubbles appear on the surface. Remove to a platter until eight crepes are made. Melt ½ cup butter in a saucepan and then add the flour and stir. Pour in milk and whisk to form a thick sauce. Season to taste with salt, pepper, and nutmeg. Add wine and allow to simmer 10 minutes. Add chicken stock and simmer 5 minutes longer. Poach celery in salted boiling water for 5 minutes to tenderize it. Drain, then combine with 2 cups of the sauce. Add 3 tablespoons of Parmesan cheese to remaining sauce. Lay crepes onto an ovenproof dish, place a heaped tablespoon of the celery and chicken mixture in the center. Fold the crepe and turn over. After filling all eight, coat with remaining cheese sauce. Sprinkle remaining cheese on top and place under the broiler to brown for about 5 minutes. Serve sprinkled with cayenne pepper and garnish with parsley. Serves 8.

Earle Traynham
Columbia

COMPANY CHICKEN

12 chicken breasts, skinned
  and boned
Garlic salt
White pepper
4 Tbs. butter
½ cup dry sherry
1 lb. mushrooms (fresh
  or large can)

2 cups chicken broth
½ cup dry white wine
12 very thin slices ham
  (preferably prosciutto)
12 slices Mozzarella cheese

Pound chicken thin. Sprinkle with garlic salt and pepper. Place slice of ham on top of each breast, then a slice of cheese. Roll up and secure with toothpick. Melt 3 tablespoons butter in heavy skillet and brown delicately. Place them in shallow, rectangular baking dish which has been greased. Pour sherry over chicken. To same skillet add 1 tablespoon butter and sauté onions until soft. Add mushrooms. Blend in flour. Gradually add broth stirring until smooth. Add wine and seasonings. Pour sauce over chicken. (At this point may be cooled, wrapped in foil and frozen if desired.) Bake covered at 350⁰ for 45 minutes if not frozen. If frozen—defrost at room temperature for 1 or 2 hours before heating and bake covered at 350⁰ for 1-1½ hours.

Mary Anne Crocker
Alexandria, Virginia

CHICKEN TETRAZZINI

1 (4 oz.) pkg. medium noodles
2 cups diced chicken (or
  turkey)
6 Tbs. fat
6 Tbs. flour
1½ tsp. salt
¼ tsp. pepper
½ tsp. celery salt
2 cups chicken stock

1 cup heavy cream, scalded
1/8 tsp. sherry flavoring
  (optional)
1 (6 oz.) can mushrooms
1/3 cup toasted slivered
  almonds
3 Tbs. minced parsley
½ cup grated Parmesan
  cheese

Cook noodles in boiling salt water until tender. Drain. Melt fat; add flour and blend. Add seasoning and stock; cook over low heat until thick, stirring constantly. Remove from heat. Stir in cream, flavoring, mushrooms sauce in greased 2-quart casserole. Top with cheese. Bake uncovered in moderate oven (350⁰) for 45 minutes. Serves 8.

Mr. & Mrs. R. D. Coble
Pensacola, Florida

CURRIED CHICKEN

Chicken (4 lbs. cut into
  serving pieces)
3 cups water
3 Tbs. parsley
1/3 cup celery
1 tsp. salt
¼ tsp. pepper
2/3 cup onions (finely
  cut)

1 cup tart apples
  (chopped)
3 Tbs. salad oil
2 Tbs. flour
1 Tbs. curry powder
¼ cup lemon juice
6-8 cups rice
1 cup cream
½ tsp. salt

Place chicken in saucepan. Add water, parsley, celery, salt and pepper. Cook rapidly until it comes to a boil, reduce heat, cover and cook slowly until chicken is tender. Remove chicken from broth and set aside. Sauté onions, cut fine and chopped tart apples in salad oil in large, heavy skillet, until golden brown. Blend in flour and curry powder. Add the chicken broth slowly, stirring constantly until smooth and thickened. Blend in lemon juice, cream, and salt. Return mixture to pan and add the cooked chicken. Let simmer 20 minutes, serve over hot fluffy rice, allowing ¾ cup rice for each serving. Serves 8 to 10. Serve with any of the following toppings: raisins which have been dipped in cinnamon and sugar, pineapple chunks, chopped crisp bacon, grated coconut, preserved ginger, cut fine, chopped peanuts, hard cooked eggs (sieved separately), chutney, and chopped green onions. For a buffet dinner, serve all the toppings, placing them in small bowls around the platter of chicken. Keep the rice hot in a chafing dish.

Mrs. Allen B. Thomas
Aiken

CURRIED CHICKEN

½ cup onions
½ cup chopped celery
4 Tbs. chicken fat
1/3 cup flour
2 cups chicken stock
1 cup tomato juice

½ tsp. Worcestershire sauce
1 tsp. curry powder
Salt and pepper to taste
4 cups diced chicken
4 cups rice

Simmer onion and celery in fat until yellow. Add flour and mix thoroughly. Add stock and cook until smooth and thick. Add tomato juice, seasoning and chicken. Mold rice into ring. Put chicken in center of rice ring.

Mrs. Alexander M. Sanders, Sr.
Columbia

ROUNTREE'S GOLDEN FRIED CHICKEN

Chicken (cut up)
Lemon (3 for each chicken)
Seasoning salt
Lemon pepper

Flour
Shortening
Cinnamon

Soak each piece of chicken in freshly squeezed lemon juice. Soak for 45-60 minutes. Completely cover in seasoning salt and lemon pepper. Preheat shortening to 350^0. Roll chicken in flour, then place in frying pan. Cook 11 minutes on each side. Sprinkle cinnamon on each side before turning.

Dennis C. Rountree
Augusta, Georgia

POLYNESIAN CHICKEN

¼ cup butter
6 chicken breasts
½ cup flour
2 tsp. salt
¼ tsp. pepper
1 green pepper (thinly
  sliced)
1 onion

1/3 cup sliced stuffed
  olives
1 can pineapple chunks
1 (10 oz.) pkg. thawed
  shrimp
1 (10 oz.) can tomato soup
¼ cup chili sauce
¼ cup pineapple juice

Melt butter in 13 inch by 9 inch pan. Roll chicken in mixture of flour, salt, pepper. Place skin side down in pan. Bake at 350⁰ for 30 minutes. Turn chicken pieces. Top with green peppers, onion rings, olives, pineapple chunks. Combine tomato soup, chili sauce, and pineapple juice. Pour over chicken. Cover pan with foil. Bake 20 minutes at 350⁰. Add shrimp on top of chicken and bake 10 minutes more uncovered.

Mrs. S. N. Trakas
Laurens

SIMON AND GARFUNKEL CHICKEN

Chicken thighs, skinned
  (or use breasts, boned,
  skinned, and flattened)
1 stick butter (melted)
Salt and pepper
Mozzarella cheese
Egg and milk mixture

Bread crumbs
1 Tbs. parsley
¼ tsp. sage
¼ tsp. rosemary
¼ tsp. thyme
½ cup white wine

Spread ½ stick melted butter over chicken and salt and pepper lightly. Wrap thighs or breasts in one slice each of Mozzarella cheese (at room temperature) and secure with a toothpick. Dip each wrapped piece in egg and milk mixture, then coat with very fine dry bread crumbs. Do this twice to each piece to coat well. Bake at 350⁰ for 30 minutes in covered dish and baste with a mixture of ½ stick melted butter, wine, parsley, sage, rosemary, and thyme. Bake another 30 minutes.

Mrs. J. D. (Rebecca) Bearden
San Antonio, Texas

POULET CHASSEUR

Breasts and thighs of young
  chickens
Cooking oil
Flour
Garlic buds (cut up)

1 cup white wine
¼ cup water
Few sprigs rosemary
Parsley

Salt and pepper breast and thighs and flour lightly. Sauté in oil until golden brown. Place skin side up in a large shallow pan with cover and add garlic buds, wine, and water. Place a few sprigs of rosemary on top. Cover pan and let chicken cook slowly in a 350⁰ oven until tender, basting occasionally with the sauce or gravy. Garnish with parsley.

Mrs. David J. Watson
Clemson

CHICKEN CHALUPAS

2 lbs. chicken breasts, chopped
1 small onion (grated)
2 small cloves garlic
1 pint sour cream
Salt
16-18 corn tortillas
Oil

1 lb. sharp cheddar (grated)
½ green pepper, thinly
  sliced
1 small can roasted green
  chili pepper (diced)
Hot pepper sauce
Paprika

Cook chicken until tender in salted water, bone and chop. Grate onion and garlic into sour cream, add salt and a little chicken broth to thin. Soften tortillas by quick frying in oil, drain on paper towels. Wrap chicken and all but one cup of cheese in tortillas. Layer in casserole. Sprinkle with green pepper and chili peppers, spread with cream mixture. Add cheese and few drops of hot sauce. Repeat until all ingredients are used, ending with sour cream. Sprinkle with paprika. Chill at least 8 hours. Bake at 350⁰ for 1 hour. Serves 6-8.

Mary Anne Crocker
Alexandria, Virginia

CAPTIVATING CASSEROLE

2 cups cooked chicken
 (diced)
1 can cream of chicken soup
 (not diluted)
¾ cup mayonnaise
1 cup diced celery
1 cup cooked rice (not
 instant rice)
1 tsp. grated onion
1 Tbs. lemon juice

1 can water chestnuts
 (sliced)
½ tsp. salt
3 hard boiled eggs (sliced)
1 cup crushed cornflakes
 (or bread crumbs)
1 stick butter

Mix the first nine ingredients together. Put half of mixture into a well-greased casserole, then a layer of hard boiled egg slices. Pour the remaining half of mixture in casserole, then a second layer of egg slices. Slowly melt one stick of butter, add crushed crumbs and use this to top the casserole. Preheat oven to 350⁰. Cook casserole for 25 minutes or till bubbly and brown. Casserole may be mixed and refrigerated for two or three days ahead then cooked when desired. Do not freeze as any dish with hard boiled egg whites becomes tough and leathery when frozen. Sliced tomatoes, creamed peas and mushrooms, and a fruit salad go nicely with this casserole.

Mrs. A. Elbert (Margaret) Adams
Greenwood

CHICKEN CASSEROLE

2 cups cooked chicken
 (remove from bones)
2 cans mushroom soup
2 cups grated sharp cheese
2 cups cooked egg noodles

1 small jar pimentos and
 juice
1 small onion (finely chopped)
Salt and pepper to season
½ cup mayonnaise (optional)

Mix all ingredients well and put in casserole dish. Place in moderate preheated oven and heat until bubbly.

Mrs. L. C. Kissam, Jr.
Orangeburg

CHICKEN SPAGHETTI

1 hen (cooked)	1 cup celery
1 qt. tomatoes	3 Tbs. Worcestershire sauce
2 cans mushroom soup	1 can tomato paste
3 large onions	Salt and pepper
2 pkgs. spaghetti	1 lb. cheese (grated)
2 bell peppers	

Boil hen and cut in medium sized pieces. Cook spaghetti; cut up vegetables and cook. Combine tomatoes and paste. Then into large sized roaster place a layer of chicken, a layer of cooked spaghetti, a layer of cooked vegetables, mushroom soup, and then tomatoes. Continue layers until all is used. Add 2 cups chicken stock. Cook in oven about 1½ hours slowly. Last 15 minutes, sprinkle cheese on top. Serves 12.

Mrs. J. D. Beard, Jr.
North Augusta

SAUSAGE AND CHICKEN CASSEROLE

1 chicken	2 cans mushrooms (drained)
1 (6 oz.) pkg. wild rice	1 can mushroom soup
1 lb. milk sausage	1 pkg. herb dressing

Cook chicken, debone, and place on bottom of casserole. Cook wild rice. Brown sausage, draining grease. Mix all ingredients together. Sprinkle herb dressing on top. Bake at 350^0 until hot.

Mrs. R. R. Rigby
Columbia

CHICKEN NEST

6 or 8 boned chicken breasts	1 can mushroom soup
1 jar chipped beef (salted)	½ pint sour cream

Mix soup and sour cream well. Form nest by folding chicken around beef. Place close together in casserole. Cover chicken and beef with soup and sour cream mixture. Cover and cook 3 hours at 350^0.

Mrs. O. K. McCarter
Tigerville

HERBED CHICKEN EN CASSEROLE

3 large chicken breasts
(cut in half)
Salt and pepper
¼ cup butter
1 can condensed cream of
chicken soup
¾ cup cooking sauterne

1 5 oz. can (2/3 cup) water
chestnuts (drained and
sliced)
1 3 oz. can (2/3 cup) broiled
sliced mushrooms (drained)
2 Tbs. chopped green pepper
¼ tsp. crushed thyme

Lightly season chicken with salt and pepper; brown slowly in butter in skillet. Arrange browned chicken, skin side up, in dish (11½ x 7½ x 1½). For the sauce, add soup to drippings in skillet; slowly add sauterne, stirring smooth. Add remaining ingredients; heat to boiling. Pour sauce over chicken. Cover with foil and bake in moderate oven (350⁰) for 25 minutes. Uncover; continue baking 25 to 35 minutes or until chicken is tender. Serve with hot fluffy rice, if desired. Makes 6 servings.

Mr. & Mrs. R. D. Coble
Pensacola, Florida

CHICKEN AND DUMPLINGS

½ of a 2 lb. chicken
(cut into pieces)
1 egg
¼ to ½ cup milk

¾ cup milk
½ tsp. salt
1½ cups all-purpose flour

Salt and pepper chicken. Place chicken in a saucepan and cover with water. Cook chicken until it is done. Then remove chicken from broth and set aside. Remove all bone, skin, and gristle from chicken.

For Dumplings

In a cup beat one egg with fork, add ¼ to ½ cup milk and ½ teaspoon salt. Measure 1½ cups flour in a mixing bowl. Stir egg and milk mixture into flour. Gradually work it in with a fork. Make into a ball. Knead and divide into two balls. Flatten out and place in refrigerator. Place wax paper between flattened dough and also around it. Leave dough chilled until ready to roll out. Roll dumplings out thin on wax paper which has a little flour sprinkled on it. Also flour ball and rolling pan for easy rolling. Cut dough into 2 inch squares. Let dumplings dry out on both sides. As soon as one side dries, turn dumplings so second side can dry. Drying time is about 45 minutes. Bring chicken broth to a boil. To keep dumplings from sticking, place a layer of dumplings in the broth and put lid on for one minute (be careful—pot may boil over), remove lid and place another layer of dumplings and put lid on for another minute. Continue until all the dumplings are used up. Add chicken meat and cook for about 10 minutes. Crack lid on pot to keep from boiling over. Add ¾ cup milk to dumplings and broth after they are done. Makes 6 to 8 servings.

Mrs. Allen B. Thomas
Aiken

CHICKEN CHOW MEIN

1 (5 lb.) hen
2 cups chopped celery
2 cups chopped onions
1 can bean sprouts
2 cans Chinese vegetables
2 cans mushrooms (stems and pieces)

1 can bamboo shoots
1 can water chestnuts
4-5 Tbs. cornstarch
2-3 tsp. sugar
5-6 Tbs. Soy sauce (or more)
Salt and pepper to taste

Cover hen with water and cook until done. Fry several pieces of bacon—enough to saute onion and celery in. Put in a large pot about 4 cups of stock (the water the hen was cooked in). Pull all the meat off the cooked chicken and cube it. Add to stock. Add the sauteed onion and celery to stock and chicken. Add bean sprouts and Chinese vegetables (drained). Add mushrooms, water chestnuts (sliced), and bamboo shoots. After it simmers for awhile, thicken with the cornstarch. Add sugar, Soy sauce, salt and pepper to taste. Bring to a boil, then turn on low. Leave on low until ready to serve. (There is a danger of sticking after the Chow Mein gets cold and then is heated too fast.) Serve over rice with Chow Mein noodles sprinkled over. Serves 12 people. Toss a mixed salad, heat some rolls, and you have a complete meal!

Mrs. James H. Pearce
Pamplico

105

LOW COUNTRY CHICKEN IN RICE

1 broiler-fryer (whole
  or cut up)
6 to 8 smoked sausage links

2 cups rice
2 tsp. curry powder
1 tsp. salt

Pressure cook and bone chicken. Save stock (2 to 2½ cups). Prepare sausage links, sliced in 2 cups water. Simmer until tender and save stock. Put rice in large saucepan along with 5 cups of reserved stock. Add curry powder and salt to stock. Add cooked boned chicken and sliced sausages. Cook for 30 minutes, stirring occasionally to prevent sticking. (If reserved stock does not yield 5 cups, use 1 chicken bouillon cube to each cup of water.) Serves 8 to 10.

Mrs. W. Gilmore Moorer
Lake City

PAT'S CHICKEN CASSEROLE

1¾ cups diced cooked chicken
1 can cream of chicken soup
  (undiluted)
½ cup slivered almonds
½ cup cracker crumbs

½ cup mayonnaise
2 hard boiled eggs
  (chopped)
1 cup celery (chopped)
1 tsp. minced onion

Mix all ingredients and pour into buttered casserole. Top with Chinese noodles, crushed potato chips or buttered bread crumbs. Bake at 350⁰ for 25 or 30 minutes.

Mrs. S. O. Underwood
Lexington, Kentucky

MOTHER'S DAY CHICKEN AND RICE CASSEROLE

1 cup raw rice
Salt and pepper
1 chicken (cut-up)

1 pkg. dry onion soup mix
1 can cream of mushroom
  soup
2 cups water

Remove skin of chicken and cut up. Place raw rice in bottom of pan (9 x 12 inches). Salt and pepper chicken pieces and place on rice. Sprinkle onion soup mix over chicken. Add cream of mushroom soup mixed with water. Cover and bake at 350⁰ for 1 hour. Makes 8 servings.

Mrs. William F. Ward, Jr.
West Columbia

SOUTHERN BARBECUE CHICKEN

2 fryers cut in quarters   1 stick margarine
   (2½ lbs. each)

Place margarine in frying pan, sear chicken quarters, necks, livers and gizzards. Do not brown chicken. Place chicken and giblets in large covered roaster, baste each with barbecue sauce. Cook covered 350⁰ for 1½ hours. Remove cover from roaster last 15 minutes of cooking time. Baste chicken again with barbecue sauce. Leave in oven a few minutes after basting. Leave enough barbecue sauce for Red Gravy.

Barbecue Sauce

2 full cups catsup   Tabasco pepper sauce
½ cup white vinegar   (to taste desired)
2 tsp. prepared mustard   ½ cup light brown sugar
2 tsp. Worcestershire sauce

Mix ingredients well, cook over low heat 5 minutes (stir while cooking). Baste chicken, use remaining for Red Gravy.

Red Gravy

Grind together liver, gizzards and meat taken from chicken necks in fine grinder. Pour drippings from cooked chicken into saucepan, add above ingredients and remaining barbecue sauce. Cook 15 minutes. Thicken with flour and water mixed. Serve on rice.

Mrs. L. Marion Gressette
St. Matthews

107

DEEP DISH DRESSING

Light muffin cornbread
  (crumbled)
Chicken broth
3 slices light bread

1 small onion (grated)
1 tsp. sage
¼ tsp. "Accent"

Mix all ingredients. Bake in casserole dish at 350⁰ until browned.

Mrs. J. D. Roberts
Raleigh, North Carolina

POULTRY DRESSING

Chicken broth
4 cups day old bread crumbs
2 cups cornbread crumbs
1 or 2 cups saltine crackers
  (crumbled)
1 cup onions (white)

1 cup celery
1 tsp. poultry seasoning
½ tsp. salt
Dash black pepper
1 egg
1 cup hot water

Mix bread, cornbread, crackers, poultry seasoning, salt, and pepper. Taste to be sure mixture is not too salty. Saute celery and onions in butter until white, not brown. Add 1 cup of broth to mixture along with water. Drain grease from remaining broth. Add broth, along with equal amount of water, to mixture. Add egg and place in oven. Bake in buttered casserole at 350⁰ for 25 to 30 minutes. Serves 6 to 8.

Mrs. Allen B. Thomas, Jr.
Aiken

TURKEY OR CHICKEN DRESSING

3 cups day old cornbread
  (crumbled)
2 cups day old biscuits
  (crumbled)
1 tsp. sage

1 small onion (chopped)
Broth
1 egg
Salt, pepper
Butter

Mix cornbread, biscuits, sage, and onion. Add broth until resembles cornbread mix. Place in refrigerator overnight. When ready to bake, add egg, salt, pepper, and bit of butter (if broth is not rich). Bake in casserole at 325^0 until brown.

Mrs. J. B. Holland, Jr.
Pickens

PECAN DRESSING

1 cup celery (in julienne
  strips 1 inch long)
2 small cans mushrooms
2 Tbs. green pepper strips
½ cup pecans (chopped)
6 olives (sliced)
2 cups bread crumbs
1 medium onion (grated)

Broth from mushrooms
2 eggs
1 tsp. margarine
1 Tbs. Lea and Perrins sauce
Pinch thyme
Pinch oregano

Sauté celery, mushrooms, and green peppers until tender. Add pecans and olives. In bowl, mix bread crumbs, onions, broth, eggs, margarine, sauce, thyme, and oregano. Combine two mixtures. Use to stuff pheasant, wild duck, or quail.

Mrs. Joseph Hutchinson
Summerville

Ham

HAM LOAF

1½ lbs. smoked ham
1½ lbs. fresh pork
1 cup bread crumbs

1 cup milk
2 eggs beaten
Pepper

Grind together twice ham and pork. Soak bread crumbs in milk for few minutes. Add eggs and pepper to taste. Mix all ingredients and pack in loaf pan. Bake at 275^0 ror 2 hours. Serves 6.

Mrs. W. Blake-Haskins
Edisto Island

HAM AND ONION CASSEROLE

2 cups chopped lean ham
  (cooked)
1 no. 2 can small whole onions
2 cups grated cheddar cheese
½ cup finely chopped celery

1 can celery soup
1 soup can water
Buttered cracker crumbs

Mix ham, cheese, drained onion, celery, soup and water until thoroughly mixed. Add salt and pepper to taste. Put in 1½ to 2 quart casserole. Top with cracker crumbs. Bake at 400^0 for 35 to 45 minutes or until crumbs are browned and casserole is thoroughly heated.

Euna Kay
Belton

HAM AND POTATO CASSEROLE

2 cups ham (diced)
4 cups potatoes
  (cooked and sliced)
2 cans cream of chicken
  or mushroom soup
Dash onion pieces

1 cup cheese (grated)
1 cup buttered cracker
  crumbs or stale potato
  chips
2 Tbs. butter

110

Grease casserole. Cover bottom with 1 cup potatoes, add layer of 1 cup ham. Repeat for 2 layers. Pour soup over. Sprinkle on cheese and crumbs. Cook at 375⁰ for 25 to 30 minutes.

Mrs. Judith C. Robinson
Clover

Pork

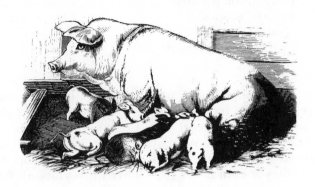

SWEET-SOUR PORK

½ tsp. salt
¼ tsp. pepper
¼ cup powdered sugar
2 Tbs. cornstarch
1 lb. lean boneless pork
  (cut into loin cubes)
2 Tbs. vegetable oil
2 Tbs. water

1 Tbs. butter or margarine
1 cup finely chopped onion
1 (8½ oz.) can diced
  bamboo shoots (drained)
Juice of 1 lemon or
3 Tbs. lemon juice
¼ cup soy sauce

In small bowl, combine salt, pepper, powdered sugar and cornstarch. Coat pork cubes with mixture. Pour oil in electric fry pan and heat, uncovered, at 325⁰. Add pork and stir-fry for 10 minutes or until evenly browned. Reduce heat to simmer. Add water, cover, and simmer for 30 minutes or until pork is fork tender. Remove cover and turn heat control to 325⁰. Push pork to the sides. Add butter. When melted, add onion and bamboo shoots and stir-fry for 2 minutes. Push to the sides. Add lemon juice and soy sauce. Reduce heat. Cook for 2 minutes. Reduce heat to warm for serving. Serve with rice or noodles. Makes 4 servings.

Josephine B. Abney
Abney Hall
Greenwood

CHOP SUEY

1½ lbs. center cut pork
  chops
1 cup celery (diced)
1 cup onion (diced)
1 can bean sprouts
  (small)
1 can water chestnuts
  (small)

1 can bamboo shoots
  (small)
Fresh or canned mushrooms
1 Tbs. soy sauce
1 tsp. sugar

Fry chopped pork until brown. Add celery, onion and other vegetables in fry pan. In large cooking pot add 2 glasses water, soy sauce, meat and vegetables. Cook until tender over medium heat. Add 1 teaspoon sugar—use grease in fry pan for flavor while cooking ingredients. Serve over white rice. Top with Chow Mein noodles or corn flakes (whichever turns you on). We love it.

Mrs. Earle Morris
Columbia

SUCCULENT PORK CHOPS

4 pocket pork chops
8 slices hard bread (or
  toast)
1 chicken bouillon cube

1 cup boiling water
¼ cup onion (finely
  chopped)
4 Tbs. butter or margarine

Buy double thick pork chops (loin only). Make a small incision on the fat side, but hollow the pork chop from one end to the other, not removing any of the meat. To make dressing, crumble bread until very fine. (The blender is excellent for this). Add onions that have been cooked in butter until soft and yellow. (Add butter, too.) Add slowly water in which bouillon cube has been dissolved. Season with salt, pepper, and a tiny bit of sage. Season to your own taste. Stuff pork chops with this dressing and bake for 1½ hours in 275⁰ or 300⁰ oven. Uncover after first hour so chops will be brown.

Mrs. James M. Graham
Hartsville

PORK CHOPS

1 large onion
 (chopped)
6 Tbs. butter
4 pork chops (thick)

1 cup white wine
2 Tbs. white wine
 vinegar
1 beef bouillon cube

Fry onions in butter. Add pork chops and brown lightly on both sides. Add ½ cup wine, cover, and simmer until done. Make sauce with pan juices, ½ cup wine, vinegar, and bouillon cube. Serve 4.

Mrs. W. Blake-Haskins
Edisto Island

DEVILED PORK CHOPS

6 medium Irish potatoes
6 medium onions
4-6 pork chops
½ cup catsup
1 Tbs. prepared mustard

2 Tbs. vinegar
1 tsp. salt
1 tsp. brown sugar
1 cup water

Peel potatoes and onions and place in deep casserole dish. Cover with pork chops. Blend remaining ingredients, then pour over pork chops. Bake at 375⁰ for 1¾ hours, basting as often as necessary.

Mrs. Heyward S. Singley
Columbia

PORK CHOP-RICE CASSEROLE

4 pork chops
1 cup rice
1 can consomme soup
1 can water
2 Tbs. oil

¼ tsp. salt
¼ cup chopped bell pepper
¼ cup chopped onions
¼ cup chopped celery

Salt and fry pork chops. Set aside. Place unwashed rice in baking dish. Add consomme, bell peppers, onion, water and celery. Stir to mix. Lay pork chops on top and cover baking dish. Bake at 400⁰ for 35 minutes or until rice is flaky and tender.

Euna Kay
Belton

ORANGE PORK CHOPS

4 pork chops, 1 inch thick
2 Tbs. flour
1 tsp. salt
¼ tsp. pepper
2 Tbs. butter or margarine

1 Tbs. brown sugar
Grated rind of 1 orange
Juice of 2 oranges
2 oranges (peeled and sliced)

Dust pork chops with flour seasoned with salt and pepper. Heat butter in heavy skillet with cover and brown chops about 5 minutes on each side. Combine sugar, orange rind and juice and pour over chops. Cover, reduce heat and simmer 40 minutes. Arrange orange slices on meat and simmer another 5 minutes. Put meat with orange slices on heated serving platter. Add 2 tablespoons water to sauce, stir, heat well and pour over meat. Makes 4 servings.

Mrs. Doris Herring
Columbia

OVEN-COOKED SPARERIBS

3 lbs. lean pork spareribs
1 cup catsup
1 Tbs. dry mustard
4 Tbs. brown sugar
1 tsp. nutmeg
1 tsp. allspice

½ tsp. cinnamon
1 tsp. salt
1 tsp. white pepper
1 small onion chopped and
 browned in a tablespoon
 of margarine

Trim and cut spareribs into serving pieces. Wash, pat dry. Lightly salt and pepper. Put into covered roasting pan. Cook for 1 hour at 300⁰. Drain after one hour and add sauce of the above listed ingredients. Coat each piece, turn over after ½ hour and coat the other side. Cook for one more ½ hour. Total cooking time, 2 hours. Serves 4.

Mrs. James M. Graham
Hartsville

LEMON BARBEQUED SPARERIBS

3½-4 lbs. lean spareribs
4 lemons (sliced thin)
1 (10 oz.) bottle Worcestershire
   sauce

Flour
Salt and pepper
Cooking oil

Remove as much fat as possible from the ribs. Salt, pepper, and flour ribs. Brown in several tablespoons of oil in frying pan. Drain oil and transfer ribs to large Dutch oven. On top of ribs, drop in sliced lemons, Worcestershire sauce and cover with water. Let simmer very slowly (covered) for 3 hours. Serve with rice and lemon gravy.

Mrs. Kitty C. Inabinet
Congaree

Miscellaneous

SAUSAGE CASSEROLE

3 to 4 cups cooked rice
1 lb. sausage
1 can mushroom soup
1 can chicken and rice
   soup
½ cup sharp cheese (grated)

Optional—but ever better
1 Tbs. onion soup mix
½ cup diced celery
¼ cup blanched almonds
1 Tbs. sherry
2 Tbs. mayonnaise

Place cooked rice in a quart casserole dish. Mix in sausage which has been cooked in a frypan, drained well, and crumbled. Stir in undiluted mushroom and chicken and rice soup. Add optional ingredients, mixing sherry with mayonnaise before adding. Add dash of black pepper and stir mixture. Top casserole with grated cheese. Bake in 350⁰ oven long enough to melt cheese and heat ingredients.

Mrs. Harris P. Smith
Easley

LAMB CURRY

1 cup raw white rice
¾ sliced onions
1 cup diced celery
1 minced peeled clove garlic
2 Tbs. fat or salad oil
1½ cups cubed leftover
cooked lamb

1 tsp. curry powder
2 cups stock from lamb
bones or lamb gravy
diluted with water
Salt
2 Tbs. flour
¼ cup cold water

Cook the rice and keep hot. Meanwhile sauté the onions, celery, and garlic in the fat in a skillet until lightly browned. Add lamb, curry powder, stock, and salt to taste. Cover, simmer 30 minutes. If necessary, thicken with the flour mixed with cold water. Sliced water chestnuts are a delightful addition. Serve in a ring of boiled rice. Serves 4. Leftover beef, veal, or pork may be substituted for the lamb. Serve as garnish shredded coconut, chopped nuts, and chutney.

Mr. & Mrs. R. D. Coble
Pensacola, Florida

LIVER CAKES

1 lb. ground pork or
beef liver
1 egg (beaten)
1 small onion (finely
chopped)

1 Tbs. flour
Salt
Pepper
Bacon strips

Mix all ingredients except bacon. Shape into patties. Wrap each with bacon strip and secure with toothpick. Fry until well done. Serves 6.

Mrs. W. Blake-Haskins
Edisto Island

VEAL WITH VEGETABLES

2 lbs. veal
½ tsp. salt
1 pkg. frozen Brussel sprouts
4 medium potatoes

1 onion
2 carrots
1 stalk celery
4 tomatoes

116

Cut meat into serving pieces. Brown in butter. Cut the onion, carrots, celery and tomatoes and add to the meat. Cover with water and cook slowly until tender. Season. Boil the Brussel sprouts and potatoes separately. Arrange on platter around meat. Make pan gravy and pour over meat.

Mrs. J. B. Traywick, II
Spartanburg

VEAL CUTLET PARMIGIANA

2 lbs. round steak (cutlet)
1 1/3 cups fine, dry bread crumbs
1/3 cup grated Parmesan cheese
3 eggs (well beaten)

1 tsp. salt
¼ tsp. pepper
1/3 cup olive oil
2 cups tomato meat sauce
6 slices (3 oz.) Mozzarella cheese

Cut steak into 6 pieces and set aside. Mix bread crumbs and Parmesan cheese. Set aside. In another bowl, combine eggs, salt and pepper. Heat olive oil in skillet. Then dip cutlets in egg mixture and then into crumb mixture. Add cutlets to skillet and brown slowly on both sides. Arrange cutlets in baking dish. Pour tomato sauce over cutlets and top with cheese slices. Bake at 350⁰ for 15 to 20 minutes or until cheese is melted and lightly browned.

Mrs. Allen B. Thomas
Aiken

Sauces

BARBECUE SAUCE

1 tsp. salt
1 tsp. chili powder
1 tsp. celery salt
1 cup catsup
½ cup water

¼ cup brown sugar
¼ cup vinegar
¼ cup Worcestershire
Few drops hot sauce
Pinch garlic powder

In saucepan, combine all ingredients. Heat on stove until hot.

Mrs. Richard (Betty) Boykin
Hampton, Virginia

BARBECUE SAUCE

1 stick margarine
1 cup catsup
½ cup vinegar
½ cup water
1 Tbs. lemon juice

2 Tbs. Worcestershire sauce
2 Tbs. Tobasco sauce
1½ Tbs. sugar
½ Tbs. salt
1½ Tbs. mustard

Melt margarine in saucepan over low heat. Add other ingredients and simmer to mix.

Mrs. William C. Mann
Seneca

BARBECUE SAUCE

2½ lbs. mustard
4 Tbs. catsup
1 tsp. Worcestershire sauce
1 Tbs. vinegar
Juice ½ lemon

Pinch sugar
Pepper
Salt
2 Tbs. butter

Beginning with mustard, blend all ingredients except butter. Melt butter in saucepan, add blended ingredients. Bring to boil. Makes ½ cup sauce.

Mrs. Allen B. Thomas
Aiken

BARBECUE SAUCE FOR CHICKEN

1 medium onion
2 Tbs. fat
2 Tbs. brown sugar
2 Tbs. vinegar
¼ cup lemon juice
1 cup catsup

3 Tbs. Worcestershire sauce
½ cup water
½ Tbs. mustard
½ cup celery (chopped)
Salt
Red pepper

Brown onions in fat. Add remaining ingredients and simmer for 30 minutes.

Mrs. James B. Edwards
Mt. Pleasant

MEXICAN BARBECUE SAUCE

1 large onion (chopped)
1 small clove garlic
  (finely cut)
½ stick butter
1 cup vinegar

2 tsp. dry mustard
1 Tbs. salt
1 Tbs. chili powder
2 cans tomato soup
½ cup water

Cook onion and garlic in butter until done. Add remaining ingredients and simmer for 5 minutes. Stir constantly.

Mrs. Jim Fleming
La Porte, Texas

MARINADE FOR RIBS

¾ cup hot water
1/3 cup soy sauce
¼ cup honey
2 Tbs. salad oil

2 Tbs. lemon juice
  (fresh, frozen, canned)
4 cloves garlic (crushed)

Combine ingredients. Marinate ribs for at least 24 hours.

Earle Traynham
Columbia

SPAGHETTI SAUCE

1 lb. ground chuck
1 large onion (chopped)
1 small bell pepper (chopped)
1 (6 oz.) can tomato paste
1 (6 oz.) can water
1 (8 oz.) can tomato sauce

½ cup catsup
1 tsp. oregano
1 tsp. parsley flakes
½ tsp. celery salt
Salt and pepper to taste

Brown ground chuck and onion. Drain in colander. Return to frypan and add all other ingredients. Simmer covered for 1 to 1½ hours.

Mrs. Lawrence R. Dixon, III
Florence

SAUCE BOYSIE

This is a recipe which my late brother gave me. He was Glenn Allan, the author of the beloved Boysie stories in the Saturday Evening Post *and of the book,* Boysie Himself.

1 cup mayonnaise (if commercial
  brand, add lemon juice and
  ½ tsp. mustard)
½ tsp. salt
½ lemon juice
2 Tbs. of any or all of the
  following:
Mushrooms (finely chopped)

Parsley
Artichoke relish
Chili sauce
Celery hearts
Green peppers
Pimentos
4 fresh green onions
  (retaining part of stalk)

Combine all ingredients. If too sour, add pinch of sugar.

Mrs. Joseph Hutchinson
Summerville

TOMATO SAUCE

12 large tomatoes
1 cup vinegar
2 Tbs. sugar

3 green pepper pods
  (chopped fine)

Boil all ingredients together until thick.

Mrs. Doris Herring
Columbia

CRANBERRY SAUCE

3 cups cranberries
1½ cups sugar

1 cup hot water

Wash cranberries and mix with sugar. Place in saucepan with water. Let stand for 5 minutes before cooking. Boil hard for 5 minutes. Let stand for 5 minutes. Boil for another 5 minutes. Allow to cool.

Kathleen Burgess
Anderson

Seafoods

SOUTH CAROLINA CATFISH STEW

Until the Great Depression, there were few South Carolinians who sought opportunities to dine on catfish. When it was served, it was usually passed rather than eaten. As a boy, I learned to cook and delight in catfish stew, cooked over a campfire in the Congaree River Swamp. On summer weekends, my friends and I would camp along Cedar Creek. After hours of conscientious hook-baiting, we usually had plenty of cats. The fish were cut crosswise in two inch sections. By the time the fish were dressed, we had fried the bacon and onions in the iron pot. The fish heads were placed on the bottom of the pot to keep the rest from sticking. Then the pieces of fish were dropped in and the pot covered over enough heat to make it simmer. Occasionally a spoon was slipped under the contents and gently raised from the bottom. (Never, never stir a catfish stew.) When the broth covered the fish, the pot was seasoned with salt, red and black pepper to taste. It was never cooked so long the fish fell off the bones. One or two eels were always added to the stew for good measure.

10 lbs. fresh catfish, dressed	Red and black pepper
3 lbs. onions, chopped	Salt
2 lbs. smoked side-meat (salt-pork)	1 can cream of mushroom soup (optional)

Fry bacon until crisp and remove. (This makes fine tidbits for your bourbon.) Fry onions in bacon fat until soft. Place fish heads in bottom of pot on onions, then add remainder of fish, occasionally raising fish gently from bottom of pot. Season to taste. If gravy appears too thin, add mushroom soup. When fish can be easily removed from the bones, the stew is done. Serves 12. Usually served with rice or grits.

Isaac Hayne, M.D.
Eastover

PEE DEE PINE BARK STEW

While catfish stew is enjoyed in one form or another throughout the Palmetto State, the concoction known as Pine Bark Stew is indigenous to the Pee Dee section. Catfish are preferred, although by no means essential. Bass will do well and even pan-fish, such as bream, redbreasts or crappie may be used. Do not use bony fish such as shad, "jack" or red-horse.

The unique name Pine Bark Stew is derived from the legendary hot seasoning of the stew. Natives of Darlington, Florence, and Williamsburg County make it so hot that one is supposed to hiccup and cry at the same time. Once upon a time, they say, a fabled Black Creek cook couldn't find any fish so he used chunks of pine bark instead. It was so infernally hot that the victims could not tell the difference. Ever since then it has been called Pine Bark Stew.

Fish	Tomato catsup
Salt bacon or fatback	Red pepper or tabasco sauce
Onions	

Fry the salt bacon until crisp enough to render a sufficient amount of clear grease. Cut up and fry several medium-sized onions until golden brown. If large fish are used, cut in sections and lay the onions so as to fill in the spaces in, around, and between the sections. If pan-fish are used, fill the cavity of each fish with the fried onions. Lay fish and onions in a deep saucepan or Dutch Oven, adding the bacon grease and sufficient water to barely cover the contents of the vessel. Bring to a boil and simmer for 10 minutes, or until able to separate fish from bone with a fork. (Caution: do not cook too long unless you want a chowder with innumerable bones mixed in.) Now add a bottle of tomato catsup and a dash of red pepper or tabasco sauce. Taste as you proceed and add salt to preferred degree. (Irish potatoes are never used in this particular stew and milk is an up-country heresy which deserves hanging.) Traditionally, this stew is served on rice with plenty of the steaming gravy.

Dr. Chapman J. Milling
Columbia

123

FISH FINGERS DELICIOUS

2 lbs. fish filets (Red Snapper) Crisco oil or peanut oil
2 eggs   Grouper, Cod, or Haddock
Corn meal   Salt

Use sharp knife and chopping board. Cut filets diagonally across grain, not more than ½ inch thick each slice. Salt these "fish fingers" to taste with plain or seasoned salt. Beat eggs and dip fish fingers into this; roll in corn meal. Fry in hot deep fat about 375^0 or 400^0 until golden brown. Drain on paper towels and keep warm until served. Serve piping hot with hush puppies and buttered grits.

Mr. Robert L. Walker
Orlando, Florida

CLAM AND CORN CASSEROLE

1¼ cups crumbled saltines   2 Tbs. chopped onions
1 cup milk   1 Tbs. chopped green pepper
2 eggs (beaten)   ½ tsp. Worcestershire sauce
1 (7½ oz.) minced clams   2 oz. sharp cheddar cheese
1 (8 oz.) can whole corn   (½ cup)
  (drained)

Mix all ingredients together. Bake at 350^0 for 50 minutes. Put cheese on top and bake for 5 more minutes. Serves 4 people.

Mrs. R. R. Rigby
Columbia

CRAB CAKES

Strom has a tremendous appetite, so I always go all out to make his meals reminiscent of the "Southern Cooking" he enjoyed when he grew up in Edgefield. Strom is very fond of seafood, and this is his favorite recipe for crab cakes.

1 lb. crab claw meat	¼ tsp. salt
2 eggs	1/8 tsp. pepper
2 Tbs. mayonnaise	Dash of Tabasco sauce
1 Tbs. Kraft's horse-raddish mustard	1 Tbs. parsley (chopped)

Combine all above ingredients including the unbeaten eggs and mix lightly together. Form mixture into desired size of cake or croquette. Do not pack firmly, but allow the mixture to be light and spongy. Roll out a package of crackers into fine crumbs (Do not use prepared cracker crumbs). Then pat the crumbs lightly on the crab cake and fry in deep fat just until golden brown. Remove hot fat just as soon as golden brown. Drain on absorbent paper and serve hot with a smile!

Mrs. Strom Thurmond
Aiken

CRAB BISQUE

½ lb. white crab meat	1 soup can of milk
½ lb. dark crab meat	½ tsp. Beau Monde
1 can cream of celery soup	(season salt)
	1 tsp. curry powder
1 can cream of mushroom soup	½ cup sherry
	Dash of Worcestershire and tabasco

Combine ingredients and heat.

Mrs. C. Frederic McCullough
Greenville

SWISS AND CRAB PIE

4 oz. natural Swiss cheese
 (shredded)
1 (9 in.) unbaked pie shell
1 (7½ oz.) can crab meat
 (drained, flaked)
2 green onions (sliced with
 tops)
3 eggs (beaten)
1 cup light cream

½ tsp. salt
½ tsp. grated lemon rind
½ tsp. dry mustard
Dash ground mace
¼ cup sliced almonds

Arrange cheese evenly over bottom of pastry shell. Top with crab meat. Sprinkle with green onions. Combine eggs, cream, salt, lemon rind, dry mustard, and mace. Pour evenly over crab meat. Top with sliced almonds. Bake in slow oven at 325⁰ for about 45 minutes or until set. Remove from oven and let stand for 10 minutes before serving. Serves 6.

Mrs. William Trakas
Madison, Wisconsin

CRAB PIE

1 lb. crab meat
4 eggs (beaten)
½ stick butter or margarine
1 stalk celery (chopped)
1 green pepper (chopped)
1 onion (chopped)
2 Tbs. minced parsley

1 cup milk
1 cup cream
1 Tbs. Worcestershire
 sauce
Dash red pepper
½ cup buttered bread
 crumbs

Sauté celery, onions and green pepper in butter or margarine until onions are clear. Add all other ingredients, after removing from heat. Pour into buttered casserole. Top with buttered bread crumbs. Bake at 325⁰ for 30 minutes or until set and brown.

Mrs. J. Lewis Wise
Aiken

CRAB—SHRIMP CASSEROLE

2 cups crab meat
2 cups shrimp (raw and
  cut up)
2 cups buttered, toasted
  bread crumbs
1 cup salad dressing

2 tsp. butter or oil
1 medium size onion
1 medium green pepper
1 cup chopped celery
½ tsp. salt
1/8 tsp. black pepper

Sauté onion, green pepper and celery in butter or oil. Add salt and pepper. Mix all ingredients together and put in baking dish. Sprinkle with paprika and bake at 350⁰ for 30 minutes.

Miss Lillian Watson
Mullins

CRAB MEAT ARVIDA

2 lbs. crab meat
½-¾ lbs. chopped-cooked shrimp
  or lobster
1½ cups mayonnaise
¼-½ cups half and half cream
1½ Tbs. chopped parsley

2 Tbs. finely chopped onion
1 Tbs. lemon-pepper seasoning
2 Tbs. lemon juice
¼ cup Harvey's Bristol
  Cream Sherry

Marinate in plastic or wooden bowl at least ½ hour. Gently mix in 8 hard-boiled chopped eggs. Place in two-quart casserole dish. Top with bread crumbs and grated Parmesan cheese. Place in 350⁰ oven for 20-30 minutes or until bubbly. Serves 8-10 people.

Mrs. John C. West
Governor's Mansion
Columbia

COASTAL DEVILED CRABS

1 lb. crab meat in chunks
2 hard boiled eggs (diced)
2 Tbs. melted butter
Juice of ½ lemon

1 tsp. prepared mustard
1/3 cups bread or cracker
   crumbs
Dash of salt

Mix crab meat, diced eggs, mustard, lemon juice and 2/3 of bread crumbs together. Place in shells or dish and pour melted butter and rest of bread crumbs on top. Bake in moderate oven 12 to 15 minutes.

Mrs. Heyward S. Singley
Columbia

DEVILISH DEVILED CRAB

1 lb. crab meat
2 eggs
½ cup cracker crumbs
1 small onion (chopped)
1 Tbs. green pepper (chopped)

1 Tbs. prepared mustard
½ cup salad dressing
1 Tbs. Worcestershire sauce
Hot sauce to taste

Mix and bake in buttered dish or crab shells. Serves 4.

Miss Lillian Watson
Mullins

TINY CRAB MEAT BALLS

2½ Tbs. flour
1/8 tsp. salt
1/8 tsp. paprika
1 Tbs. salad oil
1/3 cup milk
¼ tsp. Worcestershire sauce
1 tsp. chopped parsley

1 can (5½ oz.) crab meat
   (drained and flaked)
¾ cup fine, dry crumbs
1 egg, slightly beaten
2 Tbs. water
Cooking oil for frying

Put flour, salt and paprika in 1 quart saucepan; add salad oil; stir until smooth; add milk gradually. Cook over medium heat until mixture thickens, stirring constantly. Remove from heat; add Worcestershire sauce, parsley and crab meat; mix thoroughly.

Chill. Form into small balls (about ½ inch in diameter). Dip into crumbs, then in egg mixed with water, then in crumbs again. Fry in cooking oil about 1 minute until brown. Drain on paper towels. Serve hot with toothpick inserted in each ball. Makes about 5 dozen balls.

Mrs. Allen B. Thomas
Aiken

CRAB DIP

1 (8 oz.) pkg. cream cheese
½ cup mayonnaise
1 Tbs. lemon juice
½ tsp. Worcestershire sauce
1 tsp. all purpose flour

Dash cayenne pepper
1 (7½ oz.) can crab meat
  (drained)
1/3 cup slivered toasted
  almonds
Salt to taste

Beat cheese until smooth. Add mayonnaise, lemon juice, Worcestershire sauce, flour, and pepper. Fold in crab and almonds. Heat thoroughly. Place in chafing dish. Serve with melba toast.

Mrs. R. R. Rigby
Columbia

LOBSTER MOUSSE

1 (10¾ oz.) can tomato soup
3 (3 oz.) pkgs. cream cheese
1 cup cold water
2 Tbs. unflavored gelatin
¼ cup chopped green pepper
½ cup chopped celery
1 Tbs. minced onion

1½ cups canned lobster
1 cup mayonnaise
½ tsp. salt
¼ tsp. pepper
¼ tsp. Worcestershire sauce
Dash Tabasco sauce

Combine soup and cheese in saucepan; heat over low heat until smooth. Dissolve gelatin in water; add to soup mixture. Chill 30 to 45 minutes. Blend in remaining ingredients. Pour into mold and chill until firm. Serves 6.

Mrs. Nancy Carter
De Ridder, Louisiana

BROILED SHRIMP AND OYSTERS

1 stick butter melted
1 rounded Tbs. Cavender's
   Greek Seasoning

2 large pods garlic (mashed
   through garlic press)
2 Tbs. lemon juice
Shrimp
Oysters

Add seasoning, garlic and lemon juice to melted butter and about an hour before broiling marinate shrimp and oysters in the sauce. Place on broiler or charcoal grill until done. Baste often with butter sauce.

Mrs. Jim Fleming
La Porte, Texas

CATHERINE'S SCALLOPED OYSTERS

40 saltines
24 oz. Select Oysters (drained)
   or 36 oz. if stewing size used
1 (13 oz.) can evaporated milk

1 cup sweet milk
½ stick butter or oleo
½ tsp. salt
½ tsp. pepper

Preheat oven 350⁰. Crush crackers in bowl (not too fine), add all milk, salt and pepper, mix well (mixture will be very thin). Butter two-quart pyrex baking dish on bottom and all sides to top, put very thin layer of cracker mix on bottom. Place oysters one by one (do not over-lap them) to cover mix, dot with oleo or butter, lightly salt and pepper, then do another layer in same manner. Cover second layer of oysters with the rest of the cracker mix, spooning out carefully (as with the first and second layer.) Lightly salt and pepper and dot top with remainder of oleo or butter. Cook for one hour at 350⁰. Set baking dish inside foil-lined pan to catch overflow (bubbling) while cooking. Serve while hot. Will serve 4 as main dish or 6 to 8 as accompanying dish.

Mrs. James B. Beall
Anderson

ARTICHOKES AND OYSTERS EN CASSEROLE

1 can artichoke bottoms
2 cans artichoke hearts
½ lb. mushrooms (sauteed)
1 qt. large oysters
1 stick butter
1 bunch small green onions
  (minced)
½ cup fresh parsley
  (minced)

2 small cloves garlic
  (crushed)
½ cup browned flour
Dry white wine
2 Tbs. lemon juice
Pinch of thyme
½ tsp. monsodium glutamate
Salt, pepper, cayenne
1 unpeeled lemon
  (thinly sliced)
Paprika

Slice artichoke bottoms, place in a flat buttered casserole. Add chopped artichoke hearts. Cover with sautéed mushrooms. Cook oysters until they curl. Drain thoroughly in colander, reserving liquor. Melt butter, sauté onion, garlic until tender. Add parsley, cook a minute. Add flour, stir until smooth. Add enough white wine to oyster liquor to make 1½ cups of liquid. Add seasonings and stir constantly until quite thick. Add oysters, spoon mixture over artichokes and mushrooms. Arrange lemon slices over the top, add a dash of paprika. Bake until bubbling. This can be baked in individual ramekins with a slice of lemon in the center and a few unscraped artichoke leaves stuck around the edge to form a flower (if using fresh artichoke bottoms, you will need 4 artichokes). Bake at 350⁰ for 10 minutes. Serves 8 to 10.

Mrs. Clement F. Haynsworth, Jr.
Greenville

OYSTER STEW

1 pint oysters
1 qt. milk

3 Tbs. butter
Salt and pepper

Heat oysters slowly in their own juice until edges begin to curl. Season with salt and pepper. Add butter. Combine with scalded milk. Serve with crackers.

Mrs. J. B. Traywick II
Spartanburg

TOOGOODOO OYSTER STEW

1 cup diced smoked butts meat
  or 4 slices bacon
2 diced onions
1½ cups cream or
  evaporated milk
1½ cups milk
½ cup oyster liquor

1 Tbs. parsley
1 Tbs. sweet basil
Dash of Worcestershire
  sauce
Freshly ground black pepper
  to taste

In a large iron skillet, fry diced smoked butts meat or bacon. Remove meat and saute onions in drippings. Add remaining ingredients, stir, and simmer for 10 minutes. Add 2 or 3 pints of oysters. Heat until oysters begin to curl around the edges. Do not boil and do not add salt. Serve on hominy or in bowls for breakfast or supper. Serves 6 to 8.

Mrs. Adair M. McKoy, III
Wadmalaw Island

SALMON LOAF

1 cup salmon
1 cup cracker crumbs
¼ tsp. celery salt
¼ tsp. pepper

½ tsp. salt
2 eggs
1 cup milk
2 Tbs. butter (melted)

Mix all ingredients and pour into buttered loaf pan. Bake at 350⁰ for 30 minutes. Serves 4.

Mrs. J. B. Traywick II
Spartanburg

SALMON CROQUETTES

1 pint hot mashed Irish
  potatoes
1 can salmon

1 egg
Salt and pepper to taste
Cracker crumbs

Drain off all oil from salmon and pick out all the bones. Mix the salmon, potatoes, and seasoning thoroughly. Do not mix in the egg. Make the salmon mixture into pear-shaped balls. Dip these in the well-beaten egg, roll in cracker crumbs and fry in deep hot fat—preferably vegetable fat. Do not cook too long—just until they are a golden brown.

Ann M. Aycock
Jonesville

LEADENWAH SHRIMP SUPREME

1 onion (chopped)
½ green pepper (chopped)
1 stalk celery (chopped)
3 Tbs. olive oil
1 lb. raw peeled shrimp
1 can cream of chicken or
  mushroom soup
1 (4 oz.) can mushrooms
  (drained)

2 Tbs. dried onion soup
  mix
1 Tbs. parsley
1 Tbs. sweet basil
¼ cup sliced ripe olives
2 Tbs. sherry (or more to
  taste)

In a large skillet, sauté onion, pepper and celery in olive oil. Add shrimp. Cover and cook over medium low heat until pink, stirring often. Add soup, mushrooms, onion soup mix, parsley, basil, olives and sherry. Stir and heat well. Do not boil and do not add salt. Serve over rice and top with freshly ground pepper. Makes 6 servings. (This recipe also makes delicious stuffed green peppers by adding 3 cups of cooked rice. Mix well and stuff 6 to 8 peppers that have been cooked in boiling water for 5 minutes. Place in shallow baking pan. Top with grated cheese and cracker crumbs. Add 1 inch of water to pan and bake at 350⁰ for ½ hour.)

Mrs. Adair M. McKoy, III
Wadmalaw Island

SHRIMP THERMADOR

1 lb. cooked shrimp
½ cup sliced mushrooms
¼ cup butter, or melted
   fat
¼ cup flour
1 tsp. salt

½ tsp. dry mustard
Dash cayenne pepper
2 cups milk
Grated parmesan cheese
Paprika

Cut large shrimp in half. Cook mushrooms in butter for 5 minutes. Blend in flour and seasoning. Add milk gradually and cook until thick, stirring constantly. Stir in shrimp. Place in well greased 6-ounce custard cups. Sprinkle with cheese and paprika. Bake in hot oven 400⁰ for 10 minutes or until cheese browns. Serves 6.

Mrs. Allen B. Thomas
Aiken

SHRIMP KEY WEST

3 medium onions (chopped)
6 cloves garlic (minced)
1 cup olive oil or salad
   oil
1 (6 oz.) can tomato paste
6 or 8 bay leaves
2½ cups water

1 Tbs. salt
½ tsp. pepper
½ tsp. oregano
½ tsp. thyme
¼ tsp. saffron
1½-2 lbs. shrimp

Sauté onions and garlic in oil until yellow. Blend in tomato paste, water (a little at a time so that it does not become too thin—may not require full amount), and seasonings. Bring to a boil. Reduce heat and simmer ½ hour. Add raw shrimp. Cook 10 minutes or until shrimp becomes pink. Serve over rice combined with saffron (latter is optional).

Mr. R. D. Coble
Pensacola, Florida

LILA ROOF'S SHRIMP CASSEROLE

2 cups cooked shrimp
3 slices bread (cubed
  with shears)
1 cup whole milk
3 whole eggs—well beaten
2 Tbs. melted butter
½ cup chopped sweet
  green pepper

½ cup chopped celery
2 or 3 tsp. Worcestershire
  sauce
Salt & pepper to season well
½ tsp. dry mustard, dissolved
  in 1 Tbs. milk

Soak bread after cubing in the cup of milk. Mash with fork. Add everything else—stir well. Sprinkle top of casserole with fine bread crumbs. Dot with bits of butter. Bake for 45 minutes in 350⁰ oven. Brown the last ten minutes.

Mrs. W. J. Roof
Rock Hill

SHRIMP AND RICE CASSEROLE

During my career as dietitian at Coker College, I have served my Shrimp and Rice Casserole many, many times to many, many students. It always seemed to be a hit with them, and I hope it is for you and your guests.

1 lb. peeled and de-veined
  shrimp (boiled)
½ cup onion (chopped)
¼ cup green pepper (chopped)
½ cup mushrooms
½ stick margarine

1 Tbs. Worcestershire sauce
2 cups cooked rice
2 cups mushroom soup
Dash of tobasco

Sauté onions and peppers in the margarine until tender. Mix all ingredients together and place in a buttered baking dish. Bake at 350⁰ until thoroughly hot.

Mrs. W. A. Sumner
Hartsville

FAMILY SHRIMP CASSEROLE

6 eggs, beaten with a fork
1½ cups mayonnaise
½ cup chopped celery

2 cups grated sharp cheese
  (½ lb.)
1 cup cooked shrimp

Combine ingredients as given; bake at 350⁰ about 45 minutes. Top may be sprinkled with breadcrumbs.

Miss Martha Hearon
Bishopville

1 (no. 2) can artichoke hearts or 1 pkg. frozen artichoke hearts
  cooked by directions
1 lb. cooked shrimp
¼ lb. mushrooms
2 Tbs. butter
2 Tbs. Worcestershire sauce

¼ cup grated cheese
½ cup sherry
Salt, pepper, paprika
½ cup cream sauce

Drain artichokes and place in buttered casserole. Spread shrimp over them. Sauté sliced mushrooms and place over shrimp. Add cream sauce with seasoning. Top with cheese and paprika. Bake uncovered at 375⁰ for ½ hour. Serves 4.

Mrs. Joseph Hutchinson
Summerville

SHRIMP CREOLE

1½ lbs. shrimp
¼ cup chopped onion
¼ cup chopped celery
¼ cup chopped green pepper
1 clove garlic (finely chopped)
¼ cup bacon drippings or
  butter

3 Tbs. flour
1 tsp. chili powder
Dash of pepper
1 tsp. salt
2 cups canned tomatoes
Sherry (if desired)

Peel shrimp, remove sand, veins, and wash. Cook garlic, onion, celery, and pepper in bacon drippings until tender but not brown. Blend in flour and seasonings. Add tomatoes and cook until thickened, stirring constantly. Add shrimp and simmer uncovered for about ten minutes until shrimp are pink. Do not overcook shrimp. Sherry may be added just before serving if desired. Serve over rice.

Mrs. Wm. Jennings Bryan Dorn
Greenwood

SHRIMP CREOLE

In 1967, this recipe won a Columbia recipe contest and on Father's Day was served as the featured dish at Columbia's Sportsman Restaurant.

4 strips lean breakfast bacon
1 large brown onion (chopped)
1 large green pepper (chopped)
4 stalks celery (chopped)
2 medium cans tomatoes
2 lbs. cleaned shrimp
2 small cans chopped
  mushrooms
Salt

1 tsp. black pepper
4 dashes hot sauce
6 dashes Worcestershire
  sauce
½ cup tomato catsup
Parmesan cheese
Butter

Fry bacon and remove from skillet. Cook onion, green pepper and celery in drippings slowly, stirring until done. Add tomatoes (first removing hard cores), cleaned shrimp (cooked if you prefer), and mushrooms. Then add seasonings. Bring to a boil, then cut back to medium simmer for 1½ hours, stirring often. This should be thick, but if preferred, thin with a mixture of catsup and water. May be served over cooked rice or may be mixed with cooked rice. Pour into a large greased casserole dish. Sprinkle with Parmesan cheese and dot with butter. Heat in moderately low oven for 30 minutes before serving. If prepared a day ahead allow 1 hour for heating.

Mrs. William W. Vincent
Myrtle Beach

SHRIMP CREOLE

1½ lbs. shrimp, fresh
1 cup onions (coarsley chopped)
1 cup celery (chopped)
1 cup green pepper (chopped)
1 clove garlic (mashed with a garlic press over pot when ready to add)
¼ cup butter (melted)
1 (1 lb.) can tomatoes (mashed up with fork)

1 (10¾ oz.) can tomato soup
1 bay leaf
¼ tsp. black pepper
¼ tsp. cayenne
1 tsp. salt
1 tsp. sugar
1 Tbs. Worcestershire sauce

Peel shrimp, remove veins and wash. Cut large shrimp in half. Melt butter and sauté garlic, onion, celery, and green pepper for about 5 minutes or until tender. Add tomatoes, tomato soup, and all seasonings. Cover and simmer 5 minutes. Add shrimp and simmer uncovered about 20 minutes. Serve over cooked white rice. Serves 6.

Mrs. Allen B. Thomas
Aiken

CURRIED SHRIMP

4 Tbs. butter
1 small onion (minced)
1 green pepper (minced)
1 apple (peeled and chopped)
1 tsp. curry powder

¼ tsp. dry mustard
½ tsp. salt
½ tsp. sugar
2½ cups canned tomatoes
2 cups cooked shrimp (fresh)

Melt butter in skillet and stir in onion, green pepper, apple and dry ingredients. Cook until the onion is soft. Add the tomatoes, stir and cook until the mixture is well thickened and smooth. Add the shrimp, cover and turn down burner to low or simmer. Cook for 10 minutes. Serve on hot rice or toast. Serves 4.

Mrs. Allen B. Thomas
Aiken

CURRIED SHRIMP

1 to 1½ cups raw rice or
   2 cups minute rice
1 chicken bouillon cube
1 cup boiling water
5 Tbs. butter
½ cup minced onion
6 Tbs. flour
2 tsp. curry powder

1¼ tsp. salt
1½ tsp. sugar
¼ tsp. ground ginger
2 cups milk
3 lbs. cooked shrimp
1 tsp. lemon juice
1 small can mushrooms

Dissolve bouillon cube in water. In double boiler melt butter, add onion and simmer until tender. Stir in flour curry, salt, sugar and ginger. Gradually stir in bouillon and milk. Cook over boiling water, stirring until thickened. Add shrimp and lemon juice just before serving in center of rice ring on heated platter with any of following condiments in separate dishes: Crisp bacon bits; hard cooked eggs, mashed; chutney, avacado, diced; sautéed onion rings; spiced crab apple rings.

Mary Anne Crocker
Alexandria, Virginia

SHRIMP HURRY CURRY

1½ lbs. raw, peeled, cleaned
   shrimp, fresh or frozen
1 can (10 oz.) frozen cream of
   shrimp soup
2 Tbs. butter or margarine
1 can (10½ oz.) condensed cream
   of mushroom soup

¾ cup sour cream
1½ tsp. curry powder
2 Tbs. chopped parsley
Rice, toast points, or
   patty shells

Thaw frozen shrimp and soup. Melt butter in a 10-inch fry pan. Add shrimp and cook over low heat for 3 to 5 minutes, stirring frequently. Add the soups and stir until thoroughly blended. Stir in cream, curry powder and parsley. Heat. Serve over hot, fluffy rice, toast points, or in patty shells. Makes 6 servings.

Mr. R. D. Coble
Pensacola, Florida

SAVING GRACE SHRIMP AND MACARONI PIE

This dish was the favorite of the Men's Church Club suppers at Grace Episcopal Church in Charleston for many years. Because it is so tasty, so inexpensive, and can wait if the meal is delayed, it won itself the name Saving Grace.

½ lb. elbow macaroni
1 rounded Tbs. butter
or margarine
1½ cups grated cheddar
cheese
1 lb. medium-size shrimp

2 cups milk
1 tsp. prepared mustard
3 eggs
Paprika for garnishing
Salt and pepper to taste

Cook macaroni in boiling salted, water for 10 minutes. Drain and then stir one cup of the cheese and the mustard into hot macaroni. Keep ½ cup of the cheese to sprinkle on top of casserole. Beat eggs and then stir into macaroni mixture with the milk. Add the shrimp, and salt and pepper to taste. Turn into a buttered baking dish, top with ½ cup of grated cheese. Sprinkle on paprika and bake at 325⁰ for 30 minutes. Paprika adds color, flavor and garnish. Serves 6.

Mrs. John C. (Eva) Key
Isle of Palms

SHRIMP PIE

2 cups cooked shrimp
3 slices bread cut in
cubes
1 cup milk
3 eggs (well beaten)

2 Tbs. melted butter
1 cup chopped green pepper
and celery mixed
Salt and pepper to season
well

Soak the bread in the milk and mash it with a fork. Add the shrimp, butter, eggs and seasonings. Turn into a buttered casserole and bake in a moderate hot oven (about 350⁰) for 20 minutes.

Mrs. John Drummond
Ninety Six

SHRIMP REMOULADE

2 lbs. shrimp
½ cup olive oil
¼ cup Regina wine vinegar
¼ cup creole mustard (with
 horseradish)
1 tsp. salt
1 can anchovies (chopped
 fine)

1 cup celery hearts
 (chopped fine)
1 cup green onions
 (chopped fine)
Few sprigs chopped
 parlsey
1 (4 oz.) jar red pimentos
 (chopped)

Boil shrimp in "shrimp-boil mix" for 5 minutes, let cool in water. Peel shrimp, cut into smaller bits, and set aside. Mix next five ingredients in mixing bowl until thoroughly emulsified. If anchovies are used, include oil from anchovies in mix and omit salt. Next mix in the chopped vegetables, then the shrimp, until all particles are thoroughly covered with liquid base. Refrigerate at least 3 hours, while flavors blend. Serve on lettuce leaves. Makes 8 to 12 servings.

Mr. Robert L. Walker
Orlando, Florida

BREAKFAST SHRIMP

1 lb. small "crick" (creek)
 shrimp (raw and peeled)
3 Tbs. bacon drippings
¼ onion chopped fine

1 Tbs. parsley
Dash Worcestershire
 sauce
Freshly ground pepper
1 Tbs. sweet basil

Sauté shrimp and onion in bacon drippings over medium low heat until shrimp are pink. Add seasonings and a little water, if desired, and heat. Do not overcook. Serve over hominy and accompany with sliced fresh tomatoes for an old timey Island breakfast. This is also good sprinkled with lemon juice and served over rice for dinner. 6 servings.

Mrs. Adair M. McKoy III
Wadmalaw Island

MACARONI AND SHRIMP

1 lb. elbow macaroni
1 cup onion (chopped)
½ cup celery (chopped)
½ cup green peppers (chopped)

3 cans (8 oz.) Peter Pan shrimp
Mayonnaise
Paprika
Salt and pepper to taste

Cook macroni as directed on package. Drain in colander. Place in large bowl. Add onion, celery, pepper, shrimp, salt, and pepper. Add mayonnaise to mixture. Sprinkle top with paprika and place in refrigerator. Best when cold.

Agnes Nelson
Columbia

SHRIMP STUFFED FLOUNDER

Flounder
½ cup celery (chopped)
¼ cup green pepper (chopped)
¼ cup onion (chopped)
2 Tbs. butter
1 cup shrimp (cooked or
  thawed)

2 cups stuffing mix
¼ cup mayonnaise
1 Tbs. snipped parsley
2 Tbs. melted butter

Salt pocket in fish. Cook celery, onion, and bell pepper in 2 tablespoons butter. Stir in everything else. Stuff fish, cover with foil, and bake at 350⁰ for 1 hour. Brush with butter.

Kay N. Langley
Columbia

MARINATED SHRIMP

2½ lbs. shrimp
½ lb. celery tops
¼ cup mixed pickling spices
3½ tsp. salt
2 cups sliced onions
7 to 8 bay leaves

1¼ cups oil
¾ cup vinegar
2½ Tbs. capers and juice
2½ Tbs. celery seed
Dash of Tobasco

Boil shrimp in celery tops, mixed pickling spices, salt, onions, and bay leaves for 5 minutes. When cooled, alternate shrimp and onions with oil, vinegar, capers and juice, celery seed and Tobasco. Marinate 24 hours.

Mrs. John Drummond
Ninety Six

ISLAND SHRIMP SALAD

In a large bowl place:

2 to 3 lbs. boiled, peeled
 shrimp
1 small onion minced
3 stalks celery chopped

1 green pepper chopped
5 hard-cooked egg whites
 chopped

In another bowl mix:

1 cup mayonnaise
¼ cup sour cream
5 hard-cooked egg yolks
 mashed
1 Tbs. celery seed

3 Tbs. sweet pickle juice
1 tsp. Worcestershire sauce
½ tsp. mustard
1 tsp. sweet basil
Good dash seasoning salt
 and pepper

Place shrimp, onion, celery, pepper, and egg whites in large bowl. In another bowl, mix other ingredients. Stir latter into shrimp mixture and chill well. Serves 12. Serving idea: cut medium, peeled tomatoes into six sections (stem end down). Place on lettuce, spread wedges apart and spoon on salad. Top with pickle or olive slices.

Mrs. Adair M. McKoy, III
Wadmalaw Island

SHRIMP SALAD

½ lb. shrimp (raw)
Celery (put about ½ as much celery
 as you have shrimp) very finely cut
Mayonnaise

2 boiled eggs, cut up small
3 small pickles—finely
 cut up

Remove shells from shrimp and de-vein. Boil shrimp in a small amount of salt water. Let shrimp cool. Mix ingredients with shrimp.

Mrs. Allen B. Thomas
Aiken

143

SHRIMP SALAD SUPREME

1 lb. uncooked or frozen
  shrimp
1 (8 oz.) pkg. macaroni shells

3 stalks of celery
12 ripe pitted olives
12 green stuffed olives

Cook macaroni as directed on package and drain. Cook shrimp in the usual manner, adding bay leaf to boiling water; when tender, drain. Cut celery into small pieces. Cut olives into thin rings. Add all ingredients together, toss with Thousand Island dressing. Chill. Serves 8. (Hint: If one splits the shrimp in two, it makes it look as if the salad has twice as much shrimp.)

Mrs. James M. Graham
Hartsville

SHRIMP BUTTER

2 (5 oz.) cans shrimp
  (clean and shred very fine)
1 Tbs. onion (minced)
Juice 1 lemon

4 Tbs. mayonnaise
1¼ sticks soft butter
Large pkg. cream cheese

Combine all ingredients. Whip at low speed with mixer. Add salt to taste and turn into greased mold. Chill. Serve with crackers.

Mary Anne Crocker
Alexandria, Virginia

GREEN SHRIMP SAUCE

½ cup olive oil
½ cup Crisco oil
1 bunch young onions
½ large green pepper
Finely chopped celery

2/3 small bottle capers
3 Tbs. mustard (wet)
¼ bunch parsley
Juice 2 limes
Salt and paprika to taste

Mix all ingredients in blender. Let stand at least one day before serving.

Merle Jackson Oliver
Winter Haven, Florida

144

TUNA CASSEROLE

¾ can milk
1 can mushroom soup
1 (3½ or 4 oz.) pkg. potato
  chips (crushed)
1 (7 oz.) can tuna, flaked
  and drained

1 or 2 Tbs. minced onion
1 hard-boiled egg
4 Tbs. butter

Combine milk and soup and warm. Place layer of crushed potato chips in well-greased casserole (one and one-half quart size). Cover with half the tuna. Add half the onion, one egg sliced and half the soup and milk mixture. Repeat layers. Top with rest of potato chips and dot with butter. Bake at 350⁰ for 30 minutes. About 6 servings.

Mrs. John (Louise) Allen
Charleston Heights

DEVILED EGGS

6 eggs
1 small can tuna
4 garlic pickles (chopped)
1 medium onion (chopped)

Mayonnaise
Salt and pepper to taste
Paprika

Hard boil eggs. Then slice eggs lengthwise, removing yolks, and placing the white halves on platter. In bowl, mix yolks with tuna, pickles, onion, salt and pepper, and mayonnaise until creamy. With a spoon fill in hole of each sliced egg. Sprinkle with paprika. Yields: 12 deviled eggs.

Edward Nelson
Columbia

145

Game

BAKED SUMMER DUCK

8 to 10 dressed summer duck
2 cans cream of mushroom
  soup

2 pkg. onion soup mix
2 cans water

Combine soups and water. Mix well and pour slowly over duck in roasting pan. Cook at 325⁰ for 3 hours. Add giblets to gravy and serve with wild rice. Serves 10.

Mrs. Edward F. Eatmon
Kingstree

ORANGE BARBECUED WILD DUCK OR GOOSE

2 ducks or geese
Vinegar
Salt

1 onion
1 potato
Dash soy sauce

Clean ducks whole. After drawing, picking, singeing, and rinsing, put in milk cartons. Fill with warm water and freeze in block of ice. Thaw and soak ducks in milk solution of vinegar and salt water for 2 hours. Peel and quarter onion and potato into pot of water. Add tablespoon salt and soy sauce. Bring to slow boil. Add ducks. Cover, boil slowly for 1 hour. Remove from pot, put into cold water to cool. Halve ducks lengthwise, wash each half. Dry with paper towel. Paint each half inside and out with barbecue sauce. Barbecue over medium hot coals. If ducks have been parboiled done, only a couple of minutes cooking is needed to brown outside and heat thoroughly. If parboiled rare, barbecue more slowly, until heated thoroughly.

Barbecue Sauce

2/3 orange marmalade
1/3 prepared barbecue sauce

Dash soy sauce

Mrs. R. A. Underwood, Jr.
Dallas, Texas

DRUMMOND'S DOVE DINNER

Doves
1 stick butter
4 cups water
4 Tbs. sherry

1 medium onion (chopped)
Salt and pepper
Paprika

Gravy

3 Tbs. flour
1 pint water

Stock from doves
2 cans mushrooms (cut up)

Salt and pepper doves. Brown in approximately 1 stick of butter in Dutch oven. Add more if needed. Remove as they brown. To drippings add about 4 cups of water and sherry wine. Add chopped onion. Sprinkle doves generously with paprika and return to pot. Simmer, covered, for about 2 hours. (They should be about to fall apart.) Place doves in covered casserole with enough of the stock to keep from sticking—to be reheated in 400⁰ oven just before serving. Make gravy by shaking flour and water together in a jar. Stir into the stock in Dutch oven until thick. Add salt and pepper and mushrooms. Serve with hominy grits, tossed salad, hot biscuits and you have a real meal. I use this menu often in the fall since we have three sons whose chief hobby is bird hunting.

Mrs. John Drummond
Ninety Six

QUAIL WITH WILD RICE

8 quail
8 squares salt pork
8 large grape leaves
2 carrots (diced)
3 celery stalks (diced)
1 medium onion (diced)
3 tomatoes (diced)

1 cup white wine
1 cup chicken broth
1 Tbs. cornstarch
8 pinches sage
Salt and pepper to taste
Save livers of quail for wild rice

Place strip of pork over breast of each quail, sprinkle pinch of sage inside each quail, and wrap each bird in grape leaf, tying with string. Place in battered pan and bake at 450⁰ until half cooked (15 minutes). Remove quail, leaving juice in pan. Spread carrots, celery, onions, and tomatoes in pan with juice. Return to oven at same temperature for 10 minutes. Place quail on top of vegetables. Add chicken broth and 2/3 cup wine. Bake another 15 minutes. Remove quail, cutting strings. To sauce, add 1/3 cup wine in which cornstarch has been dissolved. Thicken for 2 or 3 minutes. Strain mixture, squeezing vegetables to remove juice. Serve quail topped with sauce, reserving 5 tablespoons for rice.

Mrs. Doris Herring
Columbia

VENISON ROAST

1 venison roast (cut preferably from loin) lightly salted, peppered, and dash of "Accent"	2 Tbs. softened butter ½ pkg. Lipton onion soup mix

Rub venison with butter. Place on heavy tin foil and pour soup mix over roast. Fold up, securing well, or bake in roasting bag. Bake in slow oven 20 minutes per pound or by directions on bag carton.

Mrs. W. Blake-Haskins
Edisto Island

VENISON ROAST

1 venison roast	2 Tbs. butter
Salt	½ pkg. onion soup mix
Pepper	

Salt and pepper roast lightly, rub with butter. Place on aluminium foil. Pour soup mix over roast. Fold tightly in foil. Bake in slow oven for 20 minutes per pound. Serves 6.

Miss Lillian Watson
Mullins

VENISON ROAST

(Good with any cut)
2 cups vinegar
2 stalks of celery (chopped)
2 carrots (chopped)

1 cup onions (chopped)
2 bay leaves
A few whole cloves

Bring to a boil. Let simmer 15 minutes, strain, cool and pour over venison. Let stand 12 to 24 hours in glass (earthen-ware or china container, never metal). Marinating tenderizes and takes away some of the gaminess. After marinating remove and lard well with strips of salt pork. Roast in 350⁰ oven, allowing 30 minutes per pound.

Venison Sauce

Use drippings in roast pan. Stir in 1 tablespoon of flour, ½ package of dehydrated onion soup, 1 onion chopped fine, ½ cup of dry red wine. Add 1 cup of water and cook until thick.

Let roast cool. Slice in thin slices. Put slices to cover bottom of casserole; sprinkle lightly with black pepper and garlic salt. Drizzle with sauce. Repeat until casserole is filled. Heat in casserole until hot through. Cover with chopped parsley after removing from oven. Make ahead and heat just before serving. Cover with aluminum foil while heating. This roast can be frozen and reheated for serving.

Mrs. Florence Hyman
Wiggins Hill Plantation
Florence

ROAST VENISON WITH GARLIC GRAVY

4 lb. venison roast
Salt and pepper
¼ cup margarine
2 Tbs. brown sugar
1 bay leaf (crumbled)

1 Tbs. vinegar
1 clove garlic
½ cup water
1/8 tsp. thyme

Sprinkle meat with salt and pepper to taste and place in roasting pan. Roast in 450⁰ oven for 30 minutes, turning several times to brown evenly. Meanwhile, melt butter, adding brown sugar and vinegar. Peel garlic, mince or put through garlic press and add. Add water and heat to boiling. Add thyme and bay leaf. Pour over roast. Reduce heat to 350⁰ and roast, basting occasionally, another hour, or until meat is done. Strain gravy in pan and serve with meat. Serves 6 to 8.

Mrs. Doris Herring
Columbia

Pickles and Relishes

CHOWCHOW PICKLE

1 large cabbage
1 qt. onions (chopped)
2 qt. bell pepper
   (chopped)
1 qt. vinegar

1 Tbs. tumeric
1 Tbs. dry mustard
½ cup brown sugar
2 qt. green tomatoes
   (chopped)

Sprinkle vegetables with salt, let stand overnight. Squeeze very dry, pour vinegar over. Add spices, simmer over low heat for short time.

Mrs. Luther B. Wimberly
Sumter

GARLIC PICKLES

1 jug (gallon) Alabama Girl Sour
   Pickle
1 whole pod garlic

1 can pimentos
5 lbs. sugar

Drain pickles and slice in rounds. Add sugar, garlic, and pimentos alternately. Let stand for three days, stirring each morning. Put in jars.

Mrs. M. R. Winton
Tampa, Florida

LILLIAN'S PEACH PICKLES

9 lbs. peaches (peeled)
3 lbs. sugar
1 tsp. whole allspice

1 stick cinnamon
1 qt. vinegar

Place peaches in enamel pan. Pour sugar, spice, and vinegar over peaches. Let stand at least 12 hours. Gradually bring to boil over medium heat, stirring with wooden spoon. Drain in colander. Boil syrup until thickened (about 30 minutes). Put peaches in jars, cover with hot syrup, seal. Yields 8 pints.

Miss Lillian Watson
Mullins

PICKLED OKRA

3 lbs. fresh pods of okra
  (2 or 3 inches long)
6 tsp. dill seed
6 small hot red peppers
6 cloves garlic
6 tsp. celery seed

6 tsp. mustard seed
2 Tbs. sugar
5 Tbs. salt
2 cups vinegar
2 cups water

Wash and drain okra. Put equal amounts of dill, pepper, garlic, celery and mustard seeds in each jar. Fill jars within ½ inch of top with okra. Mix and boil sugar, salt, vinegar and water until sugar and salt dissolves. Pour boiling hot solution over okra. Have okra covered with solution. Put dome lid on jar and screw band tight. Process 10 minutes in boiling water. Let jars stand 12 hours before removing band. Makes 6 pints.

Mrs. W. T. Crews
West Columbia

PICKLED OKRA

Okra (about 3 lbs.)
1 qt. white vinegar
1 cup water
½ cup salt

For each jar:
1 hot pepper
1 clove garlic
Sprigs of fresh dill, or
1 tsp. dill seed

Wash okra and cut away only a portion of the stem. In the bottom of each sterilized pint jar place a clove of garlic and a hot pepper. Pack the jar firmly with okra pods. Add sprigs of fresh dill or 1 teaspoon of dill seed to each jar. Bring vinegar, water and salt to a boil. Simmer 5 to 10 minutes and pour boiling hot over the okra. Seal jars. Yield: 5 to 7 pint jars.

Mrs. Lucille McMaster
Winnsboro

WATERMELON RIND PICKLES

5 lb. watermelon rind   1 gal. water
1 Tbs. slake lime

Dice watermelon rind and soak in slake lime overnight. Boil watermelon rind in water for 1 hour or until tender. Drain and add syrup.

Syrup

5 lbs. sugar   2 Tbs. allspice
4 cups vinegar   2 Tbs. cloves
1½ cups water   Whole lemon
2 Tbs. cinnamon   3 or 4 pieces whole ginger

Spices should be put in cloth in order to enhance flavor of syrup. Before adding watermelon rind, boil syrup for 5 minutes.

Mr. and Mrs. R. D. Coble
Pensacola, Florida

RELISH FOR COLD MEATS

1 Tbs. whole cloves   2 lbs. brown sugar
Stick cinnamon (broken)   1 pint vinegar
Skin muslin   2½ lbs. large raisins (seeded)

Tie cloves and cinnamon in muslin. Place in saucepan with brown sugar and vinegar. Stir until sugar dissolves. Boil for 5 minutes. Add raisins. Draw to side of fire. Cover closely. Simmer gently until raisins are plump and tender. Put in small jars.

Ann M. Aycock
Jonesville

155

BEST EVER RELISH

2 cups ground onion
2 cups ground cabbage
2 cups ground green tomatoes
6 medium bell peppers
3 medium sweet red peppers
¼ cup salt

3 cups sugar
2 tsp. celery seed
1 tsp. mustard seed
2 cups cider vinegar
1 cup water (or juice
  from vegetables)

Use medium coarse blade on grinder. Sprinkle salt on ground vegetables and let sit overnight. Rinse and drain. Combine remaining ingredients and pour over vegetables. Heat to boiling and simmer for 5 minutes. Seal in hot jars.

Mrs. Odd Thorsen
Rock Hill

FRIED WINESAPS (VIRGINIA STYLE)

1 doz. apples
1 cup sugar

4 Tbs. bacon drippings

Cut apples into eighths. Remove core particles and wash. Place bacon drippings in fry pan and heat. Add apples. Sprinkle with sugar. Cover and cook until syrup foams. Do not stir. With a fork, move apples about to ensure complete cooling. Remove cover. Lower heat. Cook until syrup is absorbed and apples appear glazed.

Margeurite M. Jervey
Powhatan, Virginia

BRANDY PEACHES

½ bushel ripe peaches
10 to 12 lbs. sugar

1 yeast cake

Scald and skin peaches. Place in 5 gallon earthen jar or crock. Add sugar. Cover. On second day, add yeast cake, dissolved in syrup. A weight is necessary to keep peaches submerged. Stir gently every few days. When peaches sink to bottom, put into jars. Ready to eat in 2 or 3 months.

Ann M. Aycock
Jonesville

PEACH CONSERVE

22 medium to large peaches
1 large can pineapple tidbits
8 cups sugar
1 lemon

1 orange
1 lb. pecans or walnuts
(chopped in small pieces)

Cut peaches in small slices, add pineapple. Add lemon and orange that have been cut very fine, peeling and all. Cook on top of stove, stirring frequently, for 3 to 4 hours. Pour into sterilized jars (8 oz. size)), seal with wax or self-sealing jar tops. Makes about 12 jars.

Mrs. James M. Graham
Hartsville

FIG PRESERVES

Figs
Sugar
Water

Cinnamon
Brandy

Select figs that are full-grown but not ripe. Peel. To every pound of fruit, add ¾ pound sugar, ½ pint water, and a cinnamon stick. Boil this mixture until figs are tender. Remove figs. Boil syrup until it adheres to wooden spoon. Return figs to syrup. Quickly boil. Allow to cool. Pour into jars, laying upon top of each a paper wet with brandy. Cover each jar tightly so that air cannot enter. Store in cool place.

Ann M. Aycock
Jonesville

CANDIED APPLES

1 stick margarine
7 or 8 medium apples
  (peeled and sliced)

1 cup sugar
1 tsp. vanilla

Melt margarine in heavy fry pan. Add apples, spread sugar over them. Cover and simmer for 25 minutes. Remove cover and continue to cook for 5 minutes or until syrup thickens. Remove from heat. Add vanilla.

Mrs. W. E. Hunt
Laurens

SPICED GRAPES

5 lbs. grapes
4 lbs. sugar
1 pint vinegar

1 Tbs. cloves
1 Tbs. allspice
1 Tbs. cinnamon

Pop the pulp from skins of grapes, then cook until the seed can be removed by running through a colander. Then add skins and weigh. Cook all together till thick like jam.

Mrs. Doris Herring
Columbia

158

Cereals, Cheeses, and Pasta

CHEESE PUDDING

12 to 14 slices diet bread
  (crusts removed)
3 cups milk

4 eggs
1 lb. sharp cheese
Salt and pepper to taste

Beat eggs well and fold into milk. Add salt and pepper. Cut crusts from bread and cut bread into very small pieces. Grate cheese. Grease a large casserole dish. Alternate layers of bread and cheese (top layer should be of cheese). Pour egg mixture over this. Leave in refrigerator overnight. Cook in 350⁰ oven for one hour. This can be used inside tomatoes and baked about 35 minutes or until golden brown. (Do not peel tomatoes.)

Mrs. Clement F. Haynsworth, Jr.
Greenville

EGG, OLIVE, AND CHEESE CASSEROLE

8 hard boiled eggs
1 small bottle pimento
  stuffed olives (drained
  and sliced)

2 cups grated cheddar
  cheese
Buttered cracker crumbs
2 cups cream sauce

Place eggs in bottom of casserole. Spread over olives, then cheese. Cover with cream sauce. Top with crumbs. Bake in 400⁰ oven for 35 to 40 minutes until crumbs are browned and casserole bubbles. Serve with ham, pork, or chicken.

Sauce

2 Tbs. melted butter
2 Tbs. flour

2 cups milk

Mix all ingredients. Stir over medium heat until thick.

Eurna Kay
Belton

160

CHEESE SOUFFLÉ

4 slices buttered bread
  (cut in cubes)
3 beaten eggs

2 cups milk
2 cups cheese (grated)
Salt, pepper

Place bread in casserole. Pour over other ingredients. Let stand 30 minutes. Bake for 30 minutes at 350⁰.

Mrs. Alfred Rawlinson
West Columbia

MACARONI PIE

¾ cup uncooked macaroni
1½ cups milk
3 eggs

¼ stick margarine
1 lb. cheese

Boil macaroni [in salted water] until tender. Drain and add margarine. Add eggs and cheese. Reserve enough cheese to garnish top. Add milk and season to taste.

Mrs. Lewin K. Platt
St. Stephen

DUNBAR MACARONI

2 small onions
2 stalks celery
1 Tbs. butter
2 cans tomatoes
1 Tbs. sugar

Salt and pepper
Chicken stock or chicken
  bouillon
Vermicelli (8 oz.)
1 lb. sharp cheese

Braise onions and celery in the butter. Add tomatoes, sugar, and salt and pepper to taste. Cover and cook 2 pieces (30 minutes). Use left-over chicken stock if available to cook vermicelli according to directions on package. Drain when done. Put vermicelli in large casserole. Pour tomato sauce over, and top with grated cheese. Bake at 350⁰ for 30 or 35 minutes.

Mrs. Thomas T. Traywick, Sr.
Cope

NOODLE PUDDING

¼ lb. wide egg noodles
¾ cup sugar
½ tsp. salt
1 stick butter
1 cup cottage cheese

½ cup sour cream
2 eggs
1 small can crushed pineapple
 (drained)
1 cup raisins

Cook noodles until tender, about 15 minutes. Drain. Melt butter. Beat eggs, adding sugar, other ingredients and noodles. Pour into lightly greased casserole. Add enough milk to keep mixture from drying out during cooking. Bake at 350⁰ for 45 to 60 minutes. Delicious with roast beef, ham, or turkey. Makes 8 generous servings.

Mrs. W. Gilmore Moorer
Lake City

FRIED RICE CANTONESE

1 cup rice
2 cups water
2 chicken bouillon cubes
4 Tbs. margarine
1 small onion (finely
 chopped)
1 small can mushrooms

1 small can water
 chestnuts (cut into slivers)
4 celery stalks (diagonally
 cut in fine pieces)
6 pork steaks
2 Tbs. soy sauce

Bake pork for 1 hour, cut into small pieces. Melt margarine in larger fry pan, add uncooked rice. Brown rice. Add onions, cook until soft and yellow. Add chicken bouillon cubes dissolved in water. Cover, cook on medium heat for ½ hour. Add mushrooms and chestnuts. After 10 minutes, add soy sauce, celery, and meat. Cook for 10 minutes. Serves 6.

Mrs. James M. Graham
Hartsville

BROWN RICE

1 stick margarine
1 small onion
1¼ cups uncooked rice

1 can consommé
1 can beef bouillon

Sauté onion in butter. Place in casserole dish with rice and other ingredients. Cook in 350⁰ oven, uncovered, for 30 minutes. Stir and cook another 30 minutes. Remove from oven and cover immediately until ready to serve.

Mrs. Charles H. Mains
Indianapolis, Indiana

NEW ORLEANS RICE

1 cup margarine
1½ cups rice (uncooked)
1 can Campbells onion soup

1 small can mushrooms
1 small can water chestnuts

Drain mushrooms and water chestnuts. Add to this juice enough water to make 1½ cups. Cut into small pieces the mushrooms and chestnuts. Melt margarine in deep skillet. Add rice and stir until rice is well covered. Add all ingredients. Mix well and cook in covered casserole in 325⁰ oven for 40 minutes. Uncover and lift around edges with a fork. Cook 40 minutes longer until rice is done.

Mrs. M. R. Winton
Tampa, Florida

RICE PUFFS

1 cup cold boiled rice
2 eggs (well beaten)

Salt to taste

Put rice through a potato ricer. Add eggs and salt. Drop by spoonfuls into hot fat. Fry until light brown and serve with maple syrup.

Mrs. Doris Herring
Columbia

MOTHER'S PINEAPPLE RICE

1½ cups rice
2 (no. 2) cans crushed pineapple
(in heavy syrup)

1½ cups white sugar
1 cup light brown sugar
½ stick butter

Cook rice until dry and fluffy. Put one half of rice into a well buttered casserole. Cover with one half of pineapple which has been well drained. Reserve the juice. Mix the sugars till well blended and sprinkle half over pineapple. Dot with half the butter. Repeat. Pour 2/3 cup pineapple juice over ingredients. Dot with remaining butter. Bake uncovered in a 325⁰ oven for 3½ hours. Check frequently. As rice cooks add the remaining juice. Do not stir or mix at any time. Serves 10.

Mrs. Margaret V. Smith
Tampa, Florida

CURRIED RICE BLEND

1 cup uncooked rice
2 chicken bouillon cubes
1½ tsp. curry powder
1 tsp. instant onion
½ tsp. salt

½ tsp. parsley flakes
½ tsp. green onion flakes
1/8 tsp. paprika
1 Tbs. dried mushrooms

To 3 cups boiling water, add this blend. Cover and steam for 45 minutes over medium heat.

Mrs. Clement F. Haynsworth, Jr.
Greenville

RICE CASSEROLE

1 cup white rice
1 can beef broth

1 can onion soup
1 stick margarine

Combine ingredients. Cover, bake at 300⁰ to 350⁰ for 1 hour.

Mrs. Marie King Anderson
Abbeville

GRITS CASSEROLE

4 cups water	1 roll garlic cheese
1 tsp. salt	¼ lb. margarine
1 cup grits	2 eggs (beaten)
Paprika	Milk

Boil grits for 5 minutes in water and salt. Add cheese and butter. Stir until dissolved. Combine milk to eggs until obtain 1 cup liquid. Add to grits mixture. Sprinkle with paprika. Bake at 325⁰ for 40 minutes.

Mrs. R. A. Underwood, Jr.
Dallas, Texas

GARLIC GRITS

Quaker Quick Grits	1 egg
1 stick butter	Milk
1 tube Kraft garlic cheese (grated)	

Cook 6 servings of grits, following instructions on box. While grits are hot, add butter. Add cheese. Beat egg and add enough milk to make 1 cup. When grits cool enough to prevent cooking egg, add milk and egg mixture. Stir well. Pour into baking dish and bake for 1 hour at 350⁰. Serve hot. Serves 6 to 10.

Mrs. Sam Rowland
Laurens

BAKED HOMINY OR GRITS

1 cup cold cooked hominy
1 egg
1 to 2 Tbs. butter

1 cup sweet milk
1 to 2 tsp. baking powder

Mash hominy until free from lumps, add well beaten egg, melted butter, milk, and baking powder. Add salt, if necessary. Mix well, and turn into well greased baking dish; dot top with butter. Bake at 360^0 about 20 minutes or until firm. Three to four servings. Serve while piping hot. More butter may be added when served if desired.

Charles E. Thomas
Greenville

HOMINY CASSEROLE

3 Tbs. fat
1 cup ground meat
2 tsp. salt
3 Tbs. salt
2 Tbs. chili powder
3 onions

2 cups water or liquid
  from hominy
1 can ripe olives
1 can hominy
1 cup grated cheese

Melt fat, brown onions and meat. Add water or hominy liquid and cook 15 minutes. Mix rest of water with flour and chili powder to make a paste. Add to meat—add hominy and olives. Put in casserole. Cover with grated cheese and heat in oven.

Alvina P. Zimmerman
Santa Fe, New Mexico

Salads
and Slaws

APPLE SALAD

3 or 4 apples (peeled and cubed)
1 cup small marshmallows
1 or 2 bananas (cut and cubed)
2 or 3 celery stalks

½ cup pecans (chopped)
¼ cup sugar
Orange or lemon juice

Soak bananas in enough orange juice or lemon juice to cover and keep them from darkening (about 10 minutes). Sprinkle sugar over all and let stand several minutes to melt sugar. Fold in enough mayonnaise to moisten. Chill in refrigerator until time to serve.

Mrs. Allen B. Thomas
Aiken

FRUIT SALAD

1 can crushed pineapple
1 can cut-up pears
  (halved)
12 cherries
¾ cup miniature marshmallows

1 cup whipped cream
2 Tbs. confectioners' sugar
1 cup mayonnaise
1 pkg. (8 oz.) cream cheese

Mix mayonnaise and softened cream cheese. Add all other ingredients; whipped cream last. Put in freezer overnight. Cut in squares. Serve on a lettuce leaf.

Mrs. J. L. Martin
West Columbia

FRUIT SALAD

1 pkg. cream cheese
1 can sweetened condensed
  milk
1 large container cool whip
½ cup lemon juice
1 small can crushed pineapple
2 (no. 2) cans fruit cocktail

2 to 3 bananas
1 cup pecans or walnut
  pieces
1 small bunch green grapes
  (if available)
1 to 2 Tbs. sherry
Shredded coconut for
  topping

Pour canned fruit into strainer and allow to drain thoroughly. In large mixing bowl, cream cheese at low mixer speed as sweetened milk is added. Blend in cool whip. Add lemon juice and sherry. Using spatula, stir in drained fruit cocktail, pineapple, sliced bananas and whole grapes. Add nuts. Mix all ingredients together and pour into a quart compote dish. Garnish top with coconut and sprinkle with cinnamon. Cover and store in refrigerator until ready to serve. Makes 6 to 8 servings when spooned out and placed in lettuce leaves.

Mrs. Harris P. Smith
Easley

DREAMY FRUIT SALAD

2 (no. 2) cans fruit cocktail mix
1 cup miniature marshmallows
1 small can mandarin oranges
2 ripe bananas, sliced
1 can pineapple tidbits

½ cup sliced almonds
1 pkg. Dream Whip
1 tsp. vanilla
1 Tbs. powdered sugar

Drain all canned fruit. While fruit is draining, whip Dream Whip adding vanilla and powdered sugar. Toss all above ingredients using the whipped Dream Whip for dressing. Chill for at least 2 hours, serve on a bed of lettuce.

Mrs. James M. Graham
Hartsville

PINEAPPLE-MARSHMALLOW SALAD

You won't have any trouble cleaning your mixing bowl—this salad is so tasty, the family will dip into it until it's spotless.

2 large cans crushed pineapple
  (drained)
1 pkg. small marshmallows
3 egg yolks

4 Tbs. white vinegar
2 Tbs. sugar
1 pint whipping cream
Chopped pecans

Whip cream, stir in drained pineapple, pecans, and marshmallows. Cook egg yolks, vinegar, and sugar until thick or jelly-like (3 or 4 minutes) stirring constantly. Cool a few minutes and stir well into mixture of whipped cream, pineapple, nuts, and marshmallows. Place in refrigerator and chill for several hours or overnight. Serves 10.

Mrs. Jewel P. M. McLaurin
Dillon

BLUEBERRY SALAD

2 pkg. black cherry Jello
2 cups boiling water
Juice 1 lemon

1 large can crushed pineapple
  (drained)
1 large can blueberries
  (drained)
1 cup chopped nuts

Mix Jello, water and lemon. Let set just enough to mix the pineapple, blueberries, and nuts. Mix well and put back in refrigerator.

Topping

8 oz. pkg. cream cheese
½ pint sour cream
½ cup sugar

1 tsp. vanilla
¼ cup milk

Mix all the above until smooth, spread evenly over top of Jello. Best when made the day before. Can be served as a salad or dessert.

Mrs. F. Joseph Hodge
Charleston

MOM'S BLUEBERRY SALAD

4 pkg. black raspberry
  gelatin
3 cups boiling water

1 (no. 2) can crushed pineapple
1 (no. 1) can blueberries
  (undrained)

Dissolve gelatin in water. Add pineapple and blueberries. Place in refrigerator.

Topping

½ cup sugar
1 cup sour cream

1 large pkg. cream cheese
½ cup mayonnaise

Blend together ingredients and serve on top of congealed gelatin.

Mrs. D. P. Wise
Orangeburg

BRIDAL CONGEALED SALAD

1 pkg. lime Jello	1½ cups ginger ale
¾ cup hot water	1 large can pears (cut-up)
1 cup marshmallows	1 can white grapes
1 large pkg. cream cheese	1 cup nuts

Dissolve Jello in hot water. Add marshmallows to mixture and dissolve. Add cream cheese, ginger ale, pears, grapes, and nuts. Refrigerate.

Mrs. O. K. McCarter
Tigerville

CONGEALED CRANBERRY SALAD

2 cups raw cranberries	1 small can (8½ oz.)
1 medium size orange	crushed pineapple, drained
1 cup celery (cut up)	2 (3 oz.) pkg. lemon or
1 cup chopped nuts	orange Jello
2 cups boiling water	2 cups sugar

Grind together cranberries and orange. Dissolve Jello and add remaining ingredients. Pour in individual molds or one large one. Let stand in refrigerator until congealed. Especially good with turkey or chicken. Serves 8 to 10.

Mrs. L. D. Bozard
Bowman

HEAVENLY BAVARIAN SALAD

1 (3 oz.) pkg. lime Jello	Dash salt
1 can crushed pineapple	1 cup marshmallows
1 cup water	1 cup cottage cheese
½ cup sugar	½ pint whipped cream

Dissolve the Jello in 1 cup boiling water. After the Jello dissolves, add the marshmallows to the hot mixture to melt them. In a bowl, combine the pineapple, sugar, salt, and cottage cheese. To this mixture add the Jello and mix. Fold in the whipped cream and put in refrigerator to congeal.

Mrs. T. Dewey Wise
Mt. Pleasant

PINEAPPLE SALAD

1 large pkg. lime Jello
1 large pkg. cream cheese
1 jar marshmallow whip

1 large can crushed pineapple
1 cup nuts

Make Jello and allow to set partially. Combine other ingredients and beat with mixer until smooth. Add nuts last. Add to Jello, mixing well.

Mrs. James B. Edwards
Mt. Pleasant

SPRING SALAD

1 pkg. apricot gelatin (6 oz.)
1 regular size can whole peeled
apricots (1 lb.)

1 can crushed pineapple
(8½ oz.)
1 can mandarin oranges
(11 oz.)

Drain juice from all the fruit, then add enough water to make four cups liquid. Heat to boiling and stir in gelatin. Cool and mix in the fruit; chill. The seed will fall right out of the apricots, then cut each in half. If you want it to be extra firm, for cutting perhaps, add just a bit of plain gelatin (about a teaspoon) that has been softened first in some of the cold liquid. Freezes well.

Mr. & Mrs. R. D. Coble
Pensacola, Florida

STRAWBERRY SALAD

2 pkg. (reg. size) strawberry
Jello
1 cup boiling water
1 (10 oz.) pkg. frozen
sliced strawberries
1 pint or 8 oz. sour cream

1 (8 oz.) can crushed
pineapple (drained)
3 large bananas (mashed
well)
1 cup chopped nuts (optional)

Dissolve Jello in water. Add strawberries, pineapple, nuts. Pour half of mixture in pan. Refrigerate until firm. Spread sour cream. Spoon remaining mixture over sour cream. Refrigerate until firm.

Mrs. Belle Scott
Clinton

UPSIDE DOWN PEAR SALAD

1 large can of pears (containing
  8 pear halves)
2 pkg. lime Jello
8 maraschino cherries

2 pkg. cream cheese (or 1
  large 8 oz. size)
¼ cup milk

Prepare Jello with only 2 cups hot water. Put in refrigerator until semi-chilled. When cream cheese is room temperature, beat in milk until of pouring consistency. Take Jello out of refrigerator, beat at fast speed until double in size, slowly add cream cheese mixture. Arrange pears in flat, long dish, flat side down, with cherries in the cavities. Pour the Jello, cream cheese mixture over pears. Put into refrigerator for 1 hour. Slice into 8 sections, serve on a leaf of lettuce. Use a dressing if desired. Serves 8. For the calorie watchers, cottage cheese may be substituted for cream cheese, and milk may be left out.

Mrs. James M. Graham
Hartsville

MOLDED BROCCOLI SALAD

2 pkg. frozen chopped broccoli
1 small cucumber (chopped)
3 or 4 small spring onions
  (chopped)
2 stalks celery (chopped)
2 cans jellied consommé
Salt
Pepper

Worcestershire sauce
Hot pepper sauce
1 large pkg. cream cheese
½ cup mayonnaise
2 pkg. plain gelatin

Cook broccoli until still crisp. Cool. Toss in chopped vegetables and sprinkle with vinegar. Mix cream cheese and mayonnaise together until smooth. Heat consommé. Add seasonings to taste and gelatin that has been soaked in ½ cup water. (Lemon juice may be added for tartness.) Blend consommé mixture into cream cheese mixture until smooth. Cool slightly and fold in vegetables. Put in large mold or individual ones and refrigerate until firm. Serve on lettuce leaves and garnish with sliced olives.

Mrs. William W. Doar, Jr.
Georgetown

TOMATO ASPIC

2 cups Tomato Juice
1 cup V-8 Juice
½ tsp. salt
1 Tbs. grated onions

1 tsp. lemon juice
½ tsp. Worcestershire sauce
Dash red pepper
2 pkgs. plain gelatin

Bring to boil all ingredients while gelatin is dissolving in ½ cup of cold water. Pour hot mixture into gelatin and stir well. Let cool and put in refrigerator to congeal.

Mrs. W. F. (Clara) Partridge, Sr.
Newberry

THREE BEAN SALAD

1 can French style green beans
1 can yellow wax beans
1 can kidney beans
1 thinly sliced onion
2/3 cup salad vinegar

1/3 cup salad oil
1 tsp. black pepper (no less)
1 tsp. salt
¾ cup granulated sugar

Mix all ingredients together, cover well, and let stand in refrigerator overnight.

Bobbi Fraser
Simpsonville

CABBAGE SALAD

1 pint vinegar
2 cups sugar
1 Tbs. mustard seed
1 Tbs. celery seed
1 Tbs. salt
½ tsp. tumeric

½ tsp. powdered mustard
1 large, firm cabbage, shredded
4 medium chopped onions
4 pieces of celery
1 large can pimento

Bring vinegar, sugar, mustard seed, celery seed, salt, tumeric, and powdered mustard to a boil. Pour over and mix with other ingredients.

Mrs. R. C. Stevenson
Greenville

CUCUMBERS IN SOUR CREAM

2 medium cucumbers   Dash pepper
1 cup sour cream   ¼ tsp. sugar
1 tsp. salt   2 Tbs. vinegar

Make sauce with above ingredients to pour over sliced cucumbers. Sprinkle with paprika.

Mrs. J. W. Waddill
Columbia

LETTUCE SALAD

2 hard boiled eggs   1 tsp. salt
1 clove garlic   ¼ cup vinegar
½ tsp. mustard   ½ cup oil
¼ tsp. pepper   1 head lettuce
½ tsp. paprika   1 onion

Rub garlic in bowl and mash egg yolks around the bowl. Mix rest of ingredients and add lettuce, onion and egg whites and toss.

Mrs. Jim Fleming
LaPorte, Texas

OKRA SALAD

Select small pods of okra. Wash well and trim stems, leaving a small portion of stem on each pod. Cook in a vegetable steamer no more than 7 minutes. Drain well and chill thoroughly. Arrange on shredded lettuce. Dress with a French dressing or with horseradish dressing. Onion rings or tomato wedges may be used to garnish the salad.

Horseradish Dressing

½ cup French dressing
1 Tbs. creamed horseradish

Blend well.

Mrs. Lucille McMaster
Winnsboro

MRS. PERRY'S POTATO SALAD

1 qt. Irish potatoes, diced
  to medium size
2 stalks celery, diced fine
1 Tbs. sugar
1 large onion, diced fine

2½ Tbs. vinegar
1/3 cup sweet mixed pickles,
  diced fine
¾ cup tart type mayonnaise
Salt and pepper to taste

Boil the potatoes until done, but not too soft and mealy. You may boil the potatoes with skins on, or cut to size after peeling the potatoes, and boil them already cut, whichever manner is preferred. After the onion, celery, and pickles are cut fine, combine with potatoes, sugar, vinegar, and mayonnaise, mixing all ingredients together thoroughly. Add salt and pepper to taste. Garnish with sliced hard-boiled eggs, and also with stuffed olives if desired.

Mrs. Christine F. Perry
Chester

DUBLIN POTATO SALAD

2 Tbs. vinegar
1 tsp. celery seed
1 tsp. mustard seed
3-4 medium large potatoes
2 tsp. sugar
1 tsp. salt
1 (12 oz.) can Armour Cooked Beef,
  chilled and cubed

¼ cup finely chopped dill pickle
¼ cup chopped green onion
2 cups finely grated cabbage
1 cup mayonnaise
¼ cup milk

176

Combine vinegar, celery and mustard seed, set aside. Meanwhile pare and cook potatoes. While potatoes are still hot, drizzle with vinegar mixture. Sprinkle with sugar and ½ teaspoon salt. Chill thoroughly. Before serving add cabbage, mayonnaise, milk and the second ½ teaspoon salt. Pour over corned beef mixture. Toss lightly.

Mrs. Earle C. Traynham, Jr.
Columbia

POTATO SALAD

3-4 medium large potatoes
2 eggs, hard boiled and
 finely chopped
3-4 strips bacon, fried
 crisp

1 medium onion, finely
 diced
Salad dressing (not mayonnaise)

Dice potatoes while raw and cook. Mix together cooked potatoes, eggs and chopped onions. Pour hot bacon drippings over the above mixture. Next add salad dressing and then bacon chips. Salt and pepper to taste. Spice with celery seeds, mustard seed and parsley flakes.

Mrs. Earle C. Traynham, Jr.
Columbia

MASHED POTATO SALAD

4 medium Irish potatoes
1 scoop butter (size of English
 walnut)
Salt, pepper to taste
¼ cup hot water

3 hard-cooked eggs
1 Tbs. vinegar
3 tsp. mustard
1 Tbs. chopped onion

Boil potatoes; mash; cream with butter, hot water, salt and pepper to taste. Put aside. In small bowl make a dressing of the 3 hard-cooked egg yolks (mashed), vinegar, mustard, chopped onion, salt and pepper to taste. Mix into the mashed potatoes. Pile into serving dish. Slice the whites of eggs (rings) and put over the top of the potato salad. Serves four to six. This can be served either hot or cold.

Miss Paulina Kerr Creed
Rock Hill

SPINACH SALAD

2/3 cup plain French dressing   1 lb. tender young spinach
3 eggs   Clove of garlic
8 slices bacon (very crisp)

Add garlic to French dressing. Hard boil eggs. Tear up spinach, discarding stems. Be sure it is very dry. Chop egg whites fine, push yolks through sieve. Remove garlic from dressing. Sprinkle egg over all. Toss thoroughly before serving. Cottage cheese is delicious added to salad.

Mrs. Clement F. Haynsworth, Jr.
Greenville

NUT-CRAB SALAD

1 cup sliced Brazil nuts   2/3 cup mayonnaise
2 (6 oz.) pkg. frozen crab   2 Tbs. lemon juice
   meat, thawed, drained   ¼ cup chili sauce
1 cup chopped celery   Salt
1 tsp. minced onion

Combine nuts, crab, celery and onion in a bowl; toss. Combine mayonnaise, lemon juice, chili sauce and salt. Mix thoroughly and pour over crab mixture. Cover bowl with aluminum foil. Refrigerate 2 hours or until serving time. Garnish with ripe olives and tomatoes, if desired. Serves 6.

Mrs. Nancy Carter
De Ridder, Louisiana

MACARONI SALAD

1 or 2 (7 oz.) cans tuna   ¼ cup green tomato or sweet
2 stalks celery, chopped   pickle, chopped
½ small onion, chopped   3 hard cooked egg whites,
½ green pepper, chopped   chopped
1 (8 oz.) pkg. macaroni

Dressing

3 hard cooked egg yolks, mashed
¾ cup mayonnaise
½ tsp. mustard
2 Tbs. pickle juice

Good dash: celery seed
garlic salt
pepper
basil
parsley flakes

Cook 1 8-oz. package elbow macaroni. Rinse with cold water, drain. Add to tuna mixture. Stir in dressing and mix well. Chill. Makes 6-8 servings.

Mrs. Adair M. McKoy, III
Wadmalaw Island

JAVA SALAD

1 (8 oz.) bottle Green Goddess
  dressing
3 cups hot cooked rice
¼ cup plumped raisins
1 Tbs. instant minced onions
2 cans fancy white albacore tuna
  (packed in spring water)
2/3 cup diagonally sliced celery

¼ cup diced green pepper
¼ cup chopped parsley
1 small bottle Major Grey's
  Chutney
1 can (small) pimento,
  drained and diced
¼–½ cup chopped peanuts or
  cashews

Mix all the above together and chill. Serve with melon wedges or peach halves on salad greens.

Mrs. Lenson W. (Helen Keels) Graves
Charleston

CURRIED SHRIMP AND PINEAPPLE SALAD

2 cups cooked, canned shrimp
2 hard-cooked eggs, chopped
½ cup salad oil
2½ Tbs. vinegar

2 tsp. lemon juice
½ tsp. curry powder
1 (1 lb.) can crushed
  pineapple, drained

Chill shrimp. Blend in eggs. Combine salad oil, vinegar, and lemon juice; pour over shrimp-egg mixture. Add curry powder and pineapple. Mix well; chill. Toss lightly before serving. Serve in lettuce cups or seashells. Serves 6.

Mrs. Nancy Carter
De Ridder, Louisiana

SALAD-SOUP FOR SUMMER

Cucumber—minced or chopped
Tomato—chopped
Onion—sliced in rings or chopped
Garlic—squeezed through garlic
  press
Yellow crook-neck squash—very
  small ones, sliced thinly

(If cucumbers are plentiful,
do not use the seed.)
Bell Pepper—chopped
Parsley—snipped very finely
Celery—finely chopped
Fresh Basil—snipped finely

Stir ingredients thoroughly. Season with salt, sugar, vinegar, salad oil, and pepper, if desired. Make at least thirty minutes before serving time and chill thoroughly. Serve in glass salad bowls as the first course. Be sure to serve the liquid, too. This can also be seasoned with salt and mayonnaise in lieu of the vinegar and salad oil.

Mrs. James H. Austin
Greenville

HOT CHICKEN SALAD

3 to 3½ lbs. chicken (boiled
  in salt water)
2 cans cream of chicken soup
1 can cream of mushroom
  soup
3 cups celery (diced)
½ cup almonds (slivered)

1 small minced onion
1 cup mayonnaise
3 Tbs. lemon juice
1 tsp. salt
6 boiled eggs (chopped)
3 cups crushed potato chips

180

Mix above ingredients except chicken and potato chips. Cut chicken into bite-size pieces and fold in. Bake at 400⁰ for 20 minutes or until bubbly hot. Sprinkle with potato chips and serve on rice or toast points. Serves 10 to 18.

Mrs. Frances Peebles Byars
Easley

CHICKEN MAYONNAISE

1 hen
4 envelopes Knox gelatin
1 cup cold water
2 cups chopped celery
2 cups mayonnaise

1½ cups cooked green peas
2 cups cooled chicken
  stock (all fat removed)
Salt and pepper

Cook hen and pick from bones. Cut up. Soften gelatin in cold water, dissolve over hot water. Combine remaining ingredients, add gelatin. Put into large mold (about 3 quarts) or small individual molds. Serve on lettuce or plain. Makes 10-12 servings.

Mrs. Rufus D. Elliott
Chattanooga, Tennessee

HAM AND VEGETABLE SALAD

1 envelope unflavored gelatin
¼ cup cold water
¾ cup boiling water
¼ tsp. salt
3 Tbs. vinegar
1 Tbs. prepared mustard

1 cup sour cream
½ cup mayonnaise
1 (17 oz.) can tiny green
  peas with onions
1 cup ham (finely diced)
¼ cup celery (diced)

Dissolve gelatin in cold water; add boiling water, salt, and vinegar. Cool slightly. Add mustard, sour cream, and mayonnaise. Beat until creamy. Chill until partially set. Fold in peas, ham, and celery. Pour into oiled mold.

Mrs. R. R. Rigby
Columbia

Salad Dressings

INSTANT BLEU CHEESE DRESSING

4 to 6 oz. Bleu Cheese
(preferred—Domestic Blue—Govganzola—Danish Blue)
Juice one lemon (more or less)
Regina Wine Vinegar (with tarragon—garlic—or plain)
Mayonnaise—to desired consistency

Use salad fork to crumble Blue Cheese in shallow bowl, add lemon juice and several dashes of wine vinegar. Stir in mayonnaise to desired consistency and taste—2 or 3 heaping tablespoons is enough. Like the sugar and cream to make coffee just right, so this is a very flexible, "do your own thing" recipe. Your cheese should be firm, moist, and full bodied, but never hard, dry or bitter. The crumbled cheese is mixed with lemon juice and vinegar (your own proportions or all of either) to a thin soupy mix. Mayonnaise adds body and flavor to your own desired consistency: Serves 6.

Mr. Robert L. Walker
Orlando, Florida

LOUISE'S ONION DRESSING

Onions
1 cup sugar
2 tsp. salt
2 tsp. pepper

2 tsp. paprika
2 tsp. dry mustard
1 cup vinegar
Salad oil

Fill a quart jar one-half full of chopped onions. Pour sugar over onions. Add salt, pepper, paprika, and mustard. Mash ingredients together mixing thoroughly. Let stand 10 minutes. Add the vinegar, then fill the rest of the quart jar with oil. Great on green salad. I also serve this dressing spooned over chilled asparagus on a bed of lettuce.

Mrs. C. W. Johnson, Sr.
Spartanburg

RUTH'S BEAN DRESSING

4 cups cold corn bread (crumbled)
1 cup cold biscuit (crumbled)
1 cup onions (chopped)
½ cup green peppers (chopped)

½ cup celery (chopped)
2 eggs (well beaten)
1 tsp. salt
1 tsp. pepper
6 cups broth from cooked lima beans (dried)

Mix all ingredients and bake for 35 minutes at 350⁰.

Ruth Frost
West Columbia

SALAD DRESSING

1 cup Wesson oil
1 cup catsup
½ cup lemon juice
½ cup vinegar
¾ cup sugar

1 tsp. salt
1 tsp. Worcestershire sauce
1 onion (cut fine)
1 clove garlic

Combine in blender and refrigerate.

Kay C. Coble
Columbia

SALAD DRESSING FOR GRAPEFRUIT

1 cup catsup
1 cup Wesson oil
3 hard boiled eggs (chopped)

1 cup pecans (chopped)
1 cup small pickled onions

Mix all ingredients, pour over grapefruit sections.

Mrs. Fred J. Hay
Dillon

Slaw

BURN COLE SLAW

½ cabbage
2 hard boiled eggs
Mayonnaise

Celery seed
Salt & pepper
Small pinch sugar

Grate cabbage, mash eggs with fork. Mix eggs and cabbage. Use mayonnaise to taste. Add celery seed, salt, and pepper to taste along with pinch of sugar. Make two hours in advance.

Mrs. Richard (Betty) Boykin
Hampton, Virginia

CHESTER SLAW

1 small head cabbage
2 large carrots, or
  3 small carrots
3 stalks celery
3 to 4 Tbs. vinegar
(depending on tart taste desired)

1 Tbs. sugar
½ cup tart type mayonnaise
1 tsp. salt (or more
  if desired)
¼ tsp. black pepper

Grate cabbage, carrots, and celery. Mix all of these grated ingredients together lightly with a fork. Next, add sugar, salt, pepper, mayonnaise, and vinegar, mixing all together thoroughly. Place in serving bowl, and if desired add an extra amount of grated carrots on top for a more colorful and appetizing dish. Sometimes, I add a small amount of sweet green pepper, also grated, to this slaw to give a little different flavor.

Mrs. Elihu Armstrong
Chester

COMPANY COLE SLAW

Large head cabbage
2 large carrots
1 (no. 2) can pineapple tidbits

1 cup small marshmallows
Salad dressing (commercial)

Shred cabbage, carrots, add pineapple and marshmallows. Thin commercial salad dressing with leftover pineapple juice and toss cole slaw.

Mrs. James M. Graham
Hartsville

GRANDMA HOLLER'S DUTCH COOKED SLAW

2 qts. finely shredded (not
  chopped or grated) cabbage
1 Tbs. lard (or vegetable
  shortening)
1 Tbs. butter or margarine
½ Tbs. salt
½ Tbs. sugar

Enough water to keep from
  sticking
½ cup sour cream (or whipping
  cream, or evaporated milk)
1 Tbs. vinegar

Steam cabbage with shortening, salt and sugar until tender, but not soft. Add cream (never commercial sour cream) and bring to almost boiling point, take from heat immediately and add vinegar just before serving (do not boil for cream will curdle). Makes 6 to 8 servings.

Mrs. A. D. (Martha) Miller
Rock Hill

ICEBOX CABBAGE SLAW

1 large cabbage	1½ tsp. salt
1 large onion, shredded	1 tsp. celery seed
1 cup vinegar	¾ cup salad oil
¾ cup sugar	

Place cabbage and onion in layers in a dish. Boil vinegar, sugar, salt, and celery seed for 2 minutes. Remove from heat; add salad oil. Bring to a boil; pour over cabbage and onion while hot. Cover tightly. Refrigerate overnight. Keeps indefinitely, if refrigerated. Yields: 10-12 servings.

Mrs. Allen B. Thomas
Aiken

MALINDA'S SLAW

3 qts. cabbage	1 pint vinegar
(approximately 1 head)	2½ cups sugar
1 large green pepper	1 tsp. mustard seed
1 small can pimento	1½ tsp. celery seed
4 medium chopped onions	1½ tsp. tumeric

Shred together the cabbage, pepper, pimento, and onion. Heat to boiling the vinegar, sugar, mustard seed, celery seed, and tumeric. Pour over shredded cabbage, pepper, and onions, and refrigerate. Later, jar up and keep in refrigerator. Good with collards, or other greens and great on top of hot dogs.

Kathleen Izlar Barton
Greenville

185

Sandwiches
and Soups

CHEESE AND TOMATO SANDWICH

6 slices bread
6 slices tomato

6 slices bacon
Grated cheese

Butter slices of bread. On each slice, place a slice of tomato, cover with grated cheese. Add a slice of bacon. Toast under broiler until bacon is crisp.

Mrs. Doris Herring
Columbia

CHESTER SANDWICHES

2 cucumbers
2 small onions
2 carrots (grated)
4 medium tomatoes (diced)
2 small bell peppers

3 Tbs. juice from
  vegetables
1 Tbs. plain gelatin
1 cup mayonnaise
Salt and pepper

Grind cucumbers, onions, and bell peppers. Save 3 tablespoons of juice. Add gelatin to juice, dissolve over hot water. Add remaining ingredients. Let stand overnight. Spread on bread.

Miss Lillian Watson
Mullins

CHESTER SANDWICHES

1 cup cucumbers
1 cup grated carrots
½ cup small bell peppers
½ cup chopped celery
½ cup onions

5 Tbs. V-8 juice
3 tomatoes (diced)
1 Tbs. plain gelatin
1 cup salad dressing
Dash Worcestershire sauce

Blend cucumbers, onions, and peppers in electric blender. Drain. Mix gelatin and V-8 juice and dissolve over hot water. Add all other ingredients.

J. C. Zinkosky
Roanoke, Virginia

187

PEAR AND RELISH SANDWICH SPREAD

1 peck pears
2 boxes raisins
3 Tbs. brown sugar
1 (no. 2½) can crushed pineapple
1 tsp. salt

1 tsp. allspice
1 tsp. cloves
1 tsp. cinnamon
1 cup vinegar

Grind pears and raisins. Mix all ingredients (except pineapple). Cook until mixture thickens (about 2 or more hours). Add water if mixture becomes too thick. Add pineapple. Pour in jars and seal.

Mrs. E. L. Bolick
Central

STEAK 'N' ONION SANDWICHES

1 medium onion, sliced
1 clove garlic, minced
1 Tbs. pure vegetable oil
1 can (8 oz.) tomato sauce
 with cheese
¼ cup water
½ tsp. sugar

¼ tsp. basil
1/8 tsp. pepper
4 cube steaks or hamburger
 patties (1 lb. hamburger)
4 slices French bread, toasted

Cook onion and garlic in oil until tender. Add tomato sauce with cheese, water, sugar, salt, basil and pepper; simmer 5 to 10 minutes. Meanwhile, fry or broil steaks to desired doneness. Place on bread slices and generously spoon sauce over. Serves 4.

Mrs. Nancy Carter
De Ridder, Louisiana

TEN-IN-ONE-SANDWICH

2 (5 oz.) jars cheese spread
¼ cup mayonnaise
1 tsp. prepared mustard
1 tsp. chopped onion

2/3 cup pitted ripe olives
1 unsliced sandwich loaf
 (long French or Italian loaf)
20-30 thin slices large
 salami

Blend four ingredients. Stir in olives. Make ½ inch slices to the bottom crust of sandwich loaf. Spread, facing side of first cut, with cheese filling, alternating every other cut. Insert 2 or 3 slices of salami in each cut. Spread nest of cheese mixture on top of loaf. Tie string around loaf, if necessary, to keep together. Brush top with melted butter. Bake at 350⁰ for 15 to 20 minutes. To serve, cut through bottom crusts. Makes 10 sandwiches.

Mrs. Earle C. Traynham, Jr.
Columbia

TUNA LOONIES (HOT SANDWICH)

1 can (6 oz.) tuna (flaked)
2 Tbs. bell pepper (chopped)
2 Tbs. onion (chopped)
2 Tbs. stuffed olives (chopped)
3 Tbs. sweet pickle (chopped)

3 hard cooked eggs
  (chopped fine)
½ cup mayonnaise
2 Tbs. lemon juice
Salt and pepper to taste

Mix ingredients and fill 10 hamburger rolls. Wrap each in foil and heat in 350⁰ oven until heated through.

Mrs. Odd Thorsen
Rock Hill

VEGETABLE SANDWICHES

¾ cup carrots
¼ cup celery
¼ cup onion
¼ cup cucumbers (unpeeled,
  if tender)
4 medium tomatoes (diced)

Salt and pepper to taste
½ cup mayonnaise
1 (8 oz.) pkg. cream cheese
  (softened to room temperature)

Grind carrots, celery, onion and cucumbers; add tomatoes, salt and pepper. Blend mayonnaise and cream cheese. Add to vegetable mixture. Refrigerate. Spread on bread.

Mrs. W. T. Crews, Sr.
West Columbia

WAFFLED SANDWICH REUBEN

12 slices rye bread
3 Tbs. prepared mustard
6 Tbs. sauerkraut
12 slices (1 lb.) corned beef

12 slices (approx. ¾ lb.)
  Swiss cheese
6 Tbs. butter

On each of 6 slices bread, spread ½ tablespoon mustard; top with 1 tablespoon sauerkraut. Arrange 2 slices corned beef and 2 slices of Swiss cheese on each, then top with remaining slices of bread. Butter outside of each sandwich, using ½ tablespoon of butter; grill until cheese begins to melt. Serves. 6.

Mrs. Nancy Carter
De Ridder, Louisiana

Soups

CHILLED ASPARAGUS SOUP

1 pkg. frozen asparagus
2 cups chicken stock
2 small spring onions, sautéed
  in butter

½ tsp. salt
1 Tbs. chopped parsley

Cook frozen asparagus according to directions on the package or use 1 can of asparagus which has been drained. Force the asparagus through a sieve. Blend with chicken stock and small spring onions which have been chopped and sautéed in butter. Simmer over low heat for 10 minutes. Add salt and chopped parsley. Chill for several hours. Garnish with sprigs of sweet basil and serve with lemon wedges.

Mrs. Lucille McMaster
Winnsboro

ICED TOMATO SOUP

1 Tbs. fresh chives
1 Tbs. fresh parsley
3 cups tomato juice

1 Tbs. lemon juice
Salt and cayenne to taste

Chop 1 tablespoon each of fresh chives and fresh parsley. Add to tomato juice which has been seasoned with lemon juice, salt and cayenne. Chill well and serve with lemon wedges.

Mrs. Lucille McMaster
Winnsboro

CHILLED CUCUMBER SOUP

5 cucumbers
4 stalks celery
1 can celery or mushroom soup
1 can milk

Sprigs of fresh parsley and
sweet basil
Seasonings as desired

Peel and slice cucumbers. Chop celery and a few sprigs of fresh parsley and sweet basil. Put into an electric blender with celery or mushroom soup and milk. When blended put into a saucepan and cook over low heat for 10 minutes. Add desired seasonings and chill for several hours. Serve garnished with sprigs of parsley, basil or mint.

Mrs. Lucille McMaster
Winnsboro

CREAM OF TOMATO BISQUE SOUP

1 large can stewed tomatoes
1 pint half and half milk
1 pint whole milk

1 pat butter
¼ tsp. baking soda

Heat quart of milk and stewed tomatoes in separate pans. After the tomatoes are warm, add baking soda, stirring carefully. After the milk is warm, add tomatoes very slowly to hot milk. After combined mixture is heated to serving temperature, add pat of butter. When butter is melted, serve. Serves 4.

Mrs. James M. Graham
Hartsville

POTATO CHEESE SOUP

3 medium potatoes
2 cups boiling water
3 cups milk
2 Tbs. butter or margarine
1 small onion (finely chopped)

2 Tbs. flour
1 tsp. salt
¼ tsp. cayenne
1 cup grated cheddar cheese

Cook potatoes in boiling water. Drain almost all of the water out and mash the potatoes coarsely. Add milk and heat to a simmer. Melt butter, add onion and simmer until onion is transparent. Add flour and seasonings. Combine with potato mixture and simmer, stirring every 5 minutes. Add cheese and beat until smooth. Serve hot, garnished with chives and crushed potato chips. Serves 4.

Earle Traynham
Columbia

SOUP FOR ALL AGES

2 lbs. stew beef
¼ cup soy sauce
2 beef bouillon cubes
2 (16 oz.) cans tomatoes
1 small can peas
½ can (7 oz.) asparagus
  (add water)
1 can okra

1 pkg. frozen chopped broccoli
2 medium onions (chopped)
3 stalks celery (with leaves)
¼ tsp. oregano
¼ tsp. rosemary
¼ tsp. lemon accent
Dash garlic salt
Pepper to taste

Simmer stew beef, soy sauce, and bouillon cubes for 1½ hours in a deep kettle, one-half full of water. Then add other ingredients and simmer several hours on low heat. Serve with buttered cornbread. Freeze leftover in small containers.

Mrs. Ethel P. Potter
Cowpens

BEEF SOUP

1½ lbs. stew beef
1 large onion (minced)
2 cups potatoes (cubed)
1 cup carrots (cubed)

½ cup elbow macaroni
1 can Campbell's tomato soup
1 stalk celery (cut fine)
Salt and pepper to taste

In a saucepan cover stew beef with water, add onion and celery. Cook beef until done. (This may be done in a pressure cooker in 10 minutes.) Add tomato soup, 1 can of water, carrots, and potatoes. Cook until carrots and potatoes are done. (This will only take 1 minute in a pressure cooker.) Add macaroni last and cook until macaroni is done. (Do not replace lid while macaroni is cooking.)

Mrs. Allen B. Thomas
Aiken

CLAM CHOWDER

3 onions
3 potatoes
1 large can evaporated milk

1 can minced clams
2 Tbs. margarine
Pepper and salt to taste

Melt margarine, add chopped onions and cook slowly until pale yellow and clear, stirring to keep from browning. Add cubed potatoes and 1 quart or more of water and cook until potatoes are tender. Add clams and juice. Last add the milk and season with pepper and salt. Do not boil, but let steep. Refrigerate, and serve small portions heated, not boiled.

Mrs. Frank L. Shannon
Winnsboro

CLAM CHOWDER

2 (8 oz.) cans (Snow's) minced clams
1 (10 oz.) can (Campbell's) cream
  of potato soup
2 medium potatoes—chopped
  into small cubes
1 medium green pepper—finely
  chopped
2 Tbs. finely chopped onion

3 Tbs. finely chopped celery
½ pint milk or half & half
(more if thinner consistency
  is required)
½ stick (2 oz.) butter or
  margarine
½ tsp. hot sauce
Salt and pepper to taste

Sauté potatoes, pepper, onion and celery in butter or margarine until only partially done—do not brown. To this mixture add the clams including juice; also add the cream of potato soup. Mix thoroughly and simmer for about one hour, stirring occasionally. Add seasonings and milk or cream then bring heat back to almost boiling point. Serve steaming hot with saltines. Makes 6 servings.

Mr. George D. Patterson
Myrtle Beach

ZIPP'S BEAN SOUP

1½ cups beans
1 Tbs. salt
1 or 2 lbs. cleaned
  shrimp or chicken
  (ham hock may be
  used here)
2½ qts. water

1 can tomatoes
1 large onion
1 clove garlic
Juice 1 lemon
1 pod green or red
  pepper

Soak beans in water with salt 3 hours overnight. Add ham, shrimp, or chicken. Salt and pepper to taste. Add water, boil slowly for 3 hours. Add tomatoes, onion, garlic, lemon juice, and pepper. Cook for 30 minutes. Serves 4 to 6.

Mrs. Thyra S. Robinson
Lake Placid, Florida

CORN VELVET SOUP

1 (8¾ oz.) can creamed corn
2 egg whites (lightly beaten)
2 Tbs. milk

2 cups canned chicken broth
1 Tbs. cornstarch (dissolved
  in 3 Tbs. canned chicken
  broth)

Five minutes before serving, heat chicken broth to boiling, add creamed corn, heat again to boiling. Add cornstarch mixture, stirring until thickened over medium heat. Add mixture of lightly beaten egg whites and milk. Stir, remove from heat, serve immediately.

Mrs. Carrie Jerome Anderson
Rock Hill

Mrs. G. H. Simpson
Lexington, Virginia

CHICKEN GUMBO SOUP

3 pints chicken broth
1 tsp. minced onion
2 Tbs. butter
1 cup chicken (diced)

1 cup tomatoes
2 cups okra
  (cut in rings)
1 cup cooked rice

Fry onion in butter. Add chicken broth, tomatoes, and okra. Simmer 30 minutes. Season, add chicken. If too thick, add more water or broth. Serve with tablespoon of rice.

Mrs. Doris Herring
Columbia

TURTLE SOUP

1 turtle
1 onion (diced)
½ cup peas (diced)
1 Tbs. pearl barley
4 qts. water

1 carrot (diced)
½ bunch celery (diced)
1 cup tomatoes
  (chopped)
Salt, pepper, parsley
  to taste

Wash turtle, cut skin loose from shell. Skin legs, neck. Remove all fat, save liver. Cut up, wash. Cook 4 hours in water. When tender, lift out meat. Add vegetables and seasoning. Cook until tender. Chop meat, add to soup.

Mrs. Doris Herring
Columbia

MEG MERRILIE'S SOUP

This is the soup with which the gipsy, Meg Merrilies, regaled Dominie Sampson—in the novel Guy Mannering *by Sir Walter Scott.*

4 lbs. venison (lean of fresh beef or mutton may be substituted)	2 partridges
	2 grouse
Salt and pepper	1 doz. small onions
4 qts. water	2 heads celery (cut small)
1 rabbit	6 sliced potatoes

Season venison or other meat with salt and pepper. Put into large pot. Pour in 4 quarts of water and boil 3 hours, skimming it well. Strain and put meat into another pot. Cut up rabbit, partridges, grouse; or one of each with a pheasant, a woodcock, or any other game more easily obtained. Season and put into soup. Add onions, celery, and potatoes. Let the soup simmer until the game is sufficiently done and all the vegetables are tender.

Ann M. Aycock
Jonesville

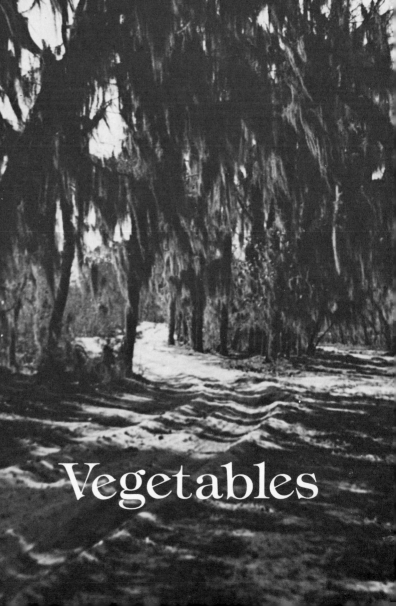

Vegetables

ARTICHOKE HEARTS WITH TOMATOES

2 Tbs. butter
3 Tbs. chopped onion
1 (no. 2) can tomatoes, drained
  and chopped

½ tsp. salt
½ bay leaf
6 to 8 canned artichoke
  hearts, drained

Sauté onions 3 to 4 minutes; add tomatoes and seasoning. Cook 10 minutes, then remove bay leaf. Place artichokes in casserole. Spoon tomatoes over. Place in 400⁰ oven 5 to 10 minutes. Makes 6 servings.

Mrs. C. Frederic McCullough
Greenville

ARTICHOKE—SPINACH CASSEROLE

10 large or 12 medium artichoke
  bottoms (not hearts)
  (use either canned or fresh
  cooked)
4 pkgs. frozen chopped spinach

1½ cans cream of mushroom
  soup
Parmesan cheese

Marinate artichoke bottoms in French dressing 3 to 8 hours. Cook 4 boxes frozen chopped spinach in salt water. Drain well. Add 1½ cans undiluted cream of mushroom soup. Sprinkle generously with Parmesan cheese. Heat. Line shallow baking dish with artichoke bottoms. Cover well with spinach mixture. Top liberally with Parmesan cheese. Bake at 350⁰ about 30 minutes or until heated through.

Mrs. John T. Robinson
New Orleans, Louisiana

ASPARAGUS SOUFFLÉ

1 can cut asparagus, drained
1 cup grated cheese
1 scant cup mayonnaise
1 can cream of mushroom soup
4 eggs

Mix all in blender. Put into buttered casserole. Put casserole in pan of hot water. Bake at 350⁰ for 1 hour.

Mrs. F. D. (Katherine) Simons, Jr.
Eutawville

ASPARAGUS CASSEROLE

1 (no. 2) can asparagus spears
2 boiled eggs
1 can cream of mushroom soup
½ cup grated cheese
(sharp cheddar)
1 cup milk
2 Tbs. butter
2 Tbs. flour

Melt butter, add flour, and blend together. Add 1 cup milk and heat. Add 1 can of cream of mushroom soup. Bring to a boil. In greased casserole, place a layer of asparagus, sprinkle with chopped eggs and grated cheese. Repeat. Pour sauce over the layers of asparagus and sprinkle with buttered bread or cracker crumbs. Bake in 375⁰ oven for 20 to 30 minutes.

Mrs. Allen B. Thomas
Aiken

MAUDE'S ASPARAGUS CASSEROLE

1 can asparagus
4 to 5 slices toasted bread
1½ cups New York sharp cheese
(grated)
Salt and pepper to taste
½ stick margarine
1 can cream of mushroom
soup

Grease casserole dish. Break some of the toast into small pieces to cover bottom of dish. Put a layer of asparagus and cheese on top of bread crumbs. Take juice from asparagus and combine in a saucepan with cream of mushroom soup. Heat and pour over first layer. Repeat procedure with another layer of bread crumbs, asparagus, cheese and sauce. Top with crumbs and pats of margarine. Bake at 350⁰ for 20 minutes.

Mrs. W. Frank Partridge, Jr.
Newberry

FRIED ASPARAGUS

1 can asparagus tips   ½ tsp. salt
2 eggs   1/8 tsp. pepper
1 cup corn flake crumbs

Drain asparagus. Beat egg, salt and pepper together. Dip each stalk of asparagus in egg, then in corn flake crumbs. Fry in fat, not too deep. Serve at once.

Mrs. Alfred Rawlinson
West Columbia

GREEN BEAN CASSEROLE

2 pkg. French style green   1 cup grated sharp cheese
  beans   1 small onion, grated
1 small can sliced mushrooms   1 can cream of mushroom soup
1 can bean sprouts   1 can cream of chicken soup
1 can water chestnuts,   1 can French-fried onions
  sliced

Mix all ingredients together except soups and French-fried onions. Place mixture in casserole in layers with soup between layers. Top with French-fried onions. Bake at 350⁰ for 45 minutes. Yields 10-12 servings.

Mrs. Ernest L. Cook
Hartsville

LIMA BEAN CASSEROLE

2 cups cooked lima beans   1 cup bread crumbs
2 Tbs. melted butter   2 Tbs. chopped green pepper
½ cup chopped nuts   ½ tsp. salt
¼ cup chopped onions   2 eggs, beaten
¼ cup light cream   Parsley (chopped)

Mix ingredients well and pour into well buttered baking dish. Bake 1 hour at 350⁰. Baste occasionally with butter and hot water mixture. Before serving sprinkle with chopped parsley. Serves 6.

Mrs. Warren B. Godbold
Wilmington, Delaware

FRIED BEANS

2 cans refried Mexican beans 4 Tbs. melted grease
2 Tbs. chopped onions

Heat grease to 375^0, sauté onions until limp, add beans, spreading them over entire fry pan. Cut heat to 325^0, cook 30 minutes or until ready to serve.

Mrs. Carrie Jerome Anderson
Rock Hill

Mrs. G. H. Simpson
Lexington, Virginia

HARVARD BEETS

1 can beets (sliced or diced) ½ tsp. salt
½ cup sugar ½ cup vinegar
1 Tbs. cornstarch 2 Tbs. butter

Mix sugar, cornstarch, salt, and vinegar in a saucepan. Boil for 5 minutes, stirring often. Add butter. Pour sauce over heated beets and let stand a few minutes before serving.

Mrs. J. B. Traywick, II
Spartanburg

STIR FRIED BROCCOLI

1 small bunch fresh broccoli
1 small onion (cut in rings)
½ cup chicken broth
½ tsp. salt

½ tsp. sugar
3 Tbs. peanut oil
1 Tsp. cornstarch
2 Tbs. chicken broth

Mix ½ cup chicken broth with salt and sugar. Mix cornstarch with 2 tablespoons chicken broth. Heat peanut oil to 400⁰, dump in broccoli and onion. Stir and turn for 3 minutes. Add chicken broth mixture, cover, turn heat to 350⁰ Cook 2 minutes, add cornstarch mixture. Stir for 1 minute. Serve immediately.

Mrs. Carrie Jerome Anderson
Rock Hill

Mrs. G. H. Simpson
Lexington, Virginia

BROCCOLI CASSEROLE

2 pkgs. frozen chopped broccoli

Sauce

1 can cream of chicken soup
½ cup mayonnaise
3 Tbs. lemon juice

Cheddar cheese (grated)
Ritz crackers
Butter

Cook broccoli slightly and drain. Mix sauce and arrange broccoli and sauce in layers. Top with grated cheddar cheese and crumbled Ritz crackers. Dot with butter. Place in casserole dish and bake at 350⁰ until hot and bubbly.

Mrs. Earle Traynham, Jr.
Columbia

ONION AND BROCCOLI CASSEROLE

6 small onions
1 pkg. frozen broccoli
2 cups white sauce (medium)

1 cup grated cheese
Paprika

Cook onions in boiling water until tender. Cook broccoli in salted boiling water. Drain both vegetables and arrange in casserole. Mix white sauce and cheese, cooking over low heat until cheese melts. Pour sauce over vegetables and sprinkle with paprika. Heat at 350⁰ until bubbly.

Mr. and Mrs. R. D. Coble
Pensacola, Florida

LIDDY'S MARINATED CARROTS

5 cups diced cooked carrots
1 medium green pepper (chopped)
2 medium onions (cut in rings)
1 can tomato soup
½ cup salad oil

1 cup sugar
¾ cup red wine vinegar
1 tsp. salt
1 tsp. pepper
1 tsp. Worcestershire sauce

Dice carrots and boil in water until almost tender. Chop pepper and onion. Combine the remaining ingredients. When carrots are done, drain, then mix all ingredients together. Refrigerate.

Mrs. Paul Murph
Whitestone

CARROTS A LA KING

4 cups diced carrots
2 cups hot medium White Sauce
1 Tbs. minced pimentos

1 Tbs. diced celery
1 Tbs. minced parsley
1 tsp. grated onion

Cook the diced carrots until tender, then drain. Meanwhile add the onion, pimentos, celery, and parsley to the hot sauce and pour over the carrots. Serves 6.

Mr. & Mrs. R. D. Coble
Pensacola, Florida

203

STEAMED CABBAGE

1½ lbs. cabbage
2 Tbs. cooking oil

2 Tbs. sugar
1 Tbs. salt

Quarter cabbage. Remove core and hard vein portion of leaves. Shred. Rinse cabbage leaves, place in heavy fry pan. Add cooking oil, sugar, and salt. (No water is needed.) Cover with lid. Bring to boil, stir. Turn back to medium heat, cook for 10 minutes. Turn off heat, allow pan to remain on burner for 15 minutes.

Mrs. J. D. Roberts
Raleigh, North Carolina

STUFFED CABBAGE

1 cabbage
2 lbs. ground beef
2 onions (chopped)
1 (no. 2) can tomatoes

1 tsp. sugar
½ cup catsup
1 cup sherry
1 small box minute rice

Sauté onions in saucepan. Add ground beef and cook until grayed. Place 12 cabbage leaves in boiling, salted water until wilted. Place in flat casserole dish and fill with meat mixture. Fold over cabbage leaves and secure with toothpicks. Sprinkle rice over cabbage leaves. Combine tomatoes, salt, pepper, sugar, catsup, and sherry. Pour over cabbage and rice and cook at 350⁰ until rice is done.

Mrs. D. P. Wise
Orangeburg

ORIENTAL CELERY

4 cups celery (cut)
5 oz. can water chestnuts
  (drained and sliced)
½ cup concentrated chicken
  soup

¼ cup toasted almonds
  (slivered)
Butter

Cook celery in boiling salted water for 8 minutes (celery should remain crisp). Drain off water. Mix in chestnuts. Toss soup, add almonds. Dot with butter over casserole. Heat in oven until bubbles.

Mrs. Clement F. Haynsworth, Jr.
Greenville

CORN PUDDING

1 can (or 2 cups fresh)
  creamed corn
3 eggs
1 Tbs. sugar
1 Tbs. salt (reduce for canned corn)

¼ tsp. pepper
1½ cups milk
2 Tbs. melted butter

Beat three eggs thoroughly, add sugar, salt, pepper and milk. Add corn and butter. Put in buttered casserole and cook at 350⁰ for 45 to 60 minutes.

Mrs. William F. Ward, Jr.
West Columbia

CORN PUDDING

This is the famous "Beaumont Inn," Harrisburg, Kentucky recipe.

2 cups corn
4 eggs
8 Tbs. flour
1 tsp. salt

2 pints milk
3 tsp. honey
2 Tbs. melted butter

Stir corn, flour, salt, honey and butter. Beat up eggs and put them in milk. Stir in corn and bake in casserole in 300⁰ oven for about 25 minutes. Stir mixture two or three times while cooking. Serves 8.

Mrs. Alfred (Mary Moon) Rawlinson
West Columbia

CORN PUDDING

1 can corn (whole kernel)
2 eggs (slightly beaten)
¼ cup sugar
1 Tbs. flour
½ stick butter

1 cup milk
Dash pepper
Dash nutmeg
½ tsp. salt

Beat eggs, add sugar and mix well. Add flour, corn (drained), butter, seasonings, and milk. Pour into casserole and cover. Cook in 400⁰ oven for 45 minutes.

Mrs. Larry H. Sharpe
Blythewood

CORN PUDDING

2 pkgs. frozen sweet corn
1 cup sweet milk
3 eggs (beaten)

½ stick butter
¼ cup sugar
Pinch salt

Mix all ingredients and cook at 325⁰ about 45 minutes or until pudding sets and is light brown on top.

Mrs. O. K. McCarter
Tigerville

FRIED CORN

3 large ears corn
3 Tbs. (heaping) flour
1 tsp. salt
2 Tbs. sugar

1/3 stick margarine
¼ tsp. pepper
½ cup water

Make 3 or 4 cuttings of the kernels off the cob (drain to the bottom of kernel). Pour into heavy frypan. Add other ingredients. Cook 10 minutes over medium heat, stirring occasionally.

Mrs. J. D. Roberts
Raleigh, North Carolina

EGGPLANT CASSEROLE

1 large eggplant
½ lb. sliced natural Swiss
  cheese (not processed)
Salt

Coarsely ground black pepper
Butter or margarine
Paprika or minced parsley

Peel and slice eggplant about 1/3 inch thick. Brown both sides gently in butter or margarine. Grease casserole, and in it alternate layers of eggplant, Swiss cheese, salt and pepper. Bottom layer should be eggplant, and top layer cheese. Cover and bake in 350⁰ oven until eggplant is tender and cheese melted—about 20 minutes. Put under broiler 2 to 3 minutes to brown, and sprinkle top with paprika and minced parsley. Serves 4-6.

Mrs. Henry M. Saalfield
Pawleys Island

EGGPLANT CASSEROLE

2 medium eggplants
1 tsp. mustard
2 eggs (beaten)
1 small bell pepper (chopped)
  or 1 onion (chopped)

1½ cups sharp grated cheese
  or more
Salt and pepper to taste

Preheat oven 350⁰. Peel eggplant, slice, and boil in salted water for 15 to 20 minutes or until tender. Drain in colander. Return to saucepan and mash. Add all other ingredients, leaving enough cheese to cover top of casserole. Put in greased baking dish, top with remaining cheese, and bake 350⁰ for about 45 minutes.

Mrs. Hammond A. Harllee
Florence

STUFFED MUSHROOMS

16 large fresh mushrooms
½ cup of fine dry bread crumbs
2 eggs (well beaten)
1 stick of oleo

1 Tbs. parsley
Dash of salt and pepper
Parmesan cheese

While washing mushrooms, remove the stems and chop very fine. Melt 2-3 tablespoons of oleo in pot and sauté chopped stems. Mix in bread crumbs, eggs, parsley, salt and pepper. Grease baking dish and arrange mushrooms cup side up. Fill each cup with stuffing and sprinkle with Parmesan cheese and a dot of oleo. Bake in a 375⁰ oven for 15-20 minutes, can be frozen until used.

Mrs. W. Frank Partridge, Jr.
Newberry

CHESTNUT—MUSHROOM CASSEROLE

2½ large (2 lb.) cans chestnuts
5 boxes fresh mushrooms
1 tsp. granulated chicken
 broth
1 can mushroom soup
2½ cups half and half

1 stick butter
4 heaping Tbs. flour
½ tsp. salt
½ tsp. white pepper
12 oz. New York State
 cheese (grated)

Make white sauce of butter, flour and cream. Add salt, pepper, broth. Add mushroom soup, sliced sautéed mushrooms, and cut up chestnuts and cheese. Heat. Serves 20.

Mrs. Clement F. Haynsworth, Jr.
Greenville

OKRA GUMBO

4 or 5 slices bacon (or ham
 chunks)
3 or 4 small onions
1 green pepper

1 (16 oz.) can tomatoes
1 (6 oz.) can V-8 Juice
1 pkg. frozen cut okra
 (or fresh equivalent)

Cut bacon into small pieces. Chop onions and green pepper into small pieces also. Sauté bacon slowly over low heat until soft (not crisp). Add chopped onions and cook slowly stirring often. When onions and bacon are sufficiently blended, add green pepper and cook until batter is soft. Add tomatoes and mix well. Add can of V-8 Juice, mix well, and cook slowly for 5 to 10 minutes. Add package of frozen cut okra and cook slowly until okra is done. Season with salt, pepper, gumbo file, rosemary, thyme, small sprinkle of Lowery's Seasoning, and a wee bit of chives if desired. Serve on rice. Will serve 4.

Mrs. Karen M. Caldwell
Spartanburg

STEAMED OKRA WITH LEMON BUTTER

Choose only very small and young okra pods. Wash well. Do not remove the entire stem, but leave a good portion of stem on each pod. Place the pods in a vegetable steamer or in a colander over boiling water. Cook exactly 7 minutes. The okra should be barely tender, very firm, and of a lovely, fresh green color. On individual serving dishes arrange the pods to resemble the spokes of a wheel. In the center of the circle of pods place a ramekin or small dish of hot butter to which lemon juice has been added. If preferred, hollandaise sauce may replace the butter. The pods are dipped into the butter and eaten in the manner of artichoke leaves.

Mrs. Lucille McMaster
Winnsboro

ZUCCHINI—EGGPLANT CASSEROLE

1 eggplant	Oregano
3 zucchini squash	Garlic powder
1 pkg. fresh mushrooms	Cheese
1 can tomato paste	Butter

Butter casserole dish. Slice and layer eggplant, zucchini and mushrooms. Mix tomato paste with equal amount of water and pour on vegetables. Sprinkle each layer with oregano and garlic powder. Top with cheese strips and dots of butter.

Jeanne Mellette
Abbeville

FRENCH-FRIED OKRA

Wash pods and remove only a portion of the stem. Dry thoroughly. If large pods are used, slice crosswise. Sprinkle with salt and pepper and dust with cornmeal. Drop into hot fat deep enough to cover the pods or slices. Fry until light brown. Serve immediately.

Mrs. Lucille McMaster
Winnsboro

GREEN PEA CASSEROLE

1 lb. can Le Seur peas,
  (drained)
1 (5 oz.) can water chesnuts
1 medium onion (chopped)

2 oz. jar chopped pimento
1 can cream of mushroom
  soup
½ cup grated cheese

Mix all together but cheese. Pour into greased 1½ quart casserole. Sprinkle cheese over all. Crouton either 4 slices of bread or crush 1 cup Ritz crackers and combine with ¾ stick melted margarine. Spread on top and bake 15 minutes at 400⁰ .

Mrs. J. L. Martin
West Columbia

HOPPIN JOHN

2 cups ham (cooked)
  and diced)
2 cups pork (cooked
  and diced)
2 cups black-eyed
  peas (frozen or canned)

4 strips bacon
  (drippings only)
2 cups rice

Cook peas with bacon drippings for 1 hour, using plenty of water. Add meats and more water. Boil for 5 minutes. Be sure to have at least 2 cups liquid. Add rice, stir. Place in greased casserole. Cover lightly with aluminum foil, steam for 1 to 1½ hours. Start at 400⁰ , reduce to 250⁰ in ½ hour.

Mrs. William W. Vincent
Myrtle Beach

HOPPIN JOHN

This is a traditional New Year's Day good luck dish. I've eaten Hoppin John on New Year's Day for thirty years.

1 cup rice
1 medium onion
1 cup blackeyed peas

Slab of bacon
Salt and pepper

Soak peas overnight. Cook peas in salt water with bacon slab. When peas are done, cook rice in steamer with minced onions and bacon. Add liquid that the peas were cooked in, then add peas. (If not enough liquid, add water.) Add salt and pepper to taste and cook 60 to 90 minutes. Serves 6.

Mrs. Richard (Betty) Boykin
Hampton, Virginia

POTLUCK BLACKEYED PEAS

¼ lb. bacon, diced
2 cups chopped celery
2 cups green pepper

2 cups chopped onion
2 cans (1 lb. each) tomatoes
2 cans blackeyed peas

Saute bacon with celery, green pepper and onion. Add tomatoes and peas. Simmer 30 to 40 minutes. Serve with jalapeno cornbread.

Mrs. R. A. Underwood, Jr.
Dallas, Texas

WHITE POTATO CASSEROLE

3 large white potatoes
¾ stick margarine

Salt and pepper

Peel and slice potatoes and place in casserole dish. Dot with margarine and sprinkle layers with salt and pepper. Cover and place in oven at 400° for one hour. This is a perfect supplement to pork chops, fish, or steak.

Mrs. Jewell P. McLaurin
Dillon

211

DUTCH FRIED POTATOES

4 medium potatoes
1 medium onion
2 cups milk
4 Tbs. flour

¾ cup shortening
(bacon drippings are better)
Salt and pepper

Peel and slice potatoes about one quarter inch thick. Place these in an average size skillet where the shortening has heated enough to fry at medium temperature. Sprinkle with a heaping teaspoon of salt (go lighter if using bacon drippings) and stir to dissolve salt through potatoes. Turn these over every 3 or 4 minutes so they can all cook tender; will take about 15 or 20 minutes, a shorter time if covered. It's not necessary for the potatoes to brown and it makes no difference if they break up somewhat. When the potatoes are done push some from an edge of the pan and put in diced onion to sauté for 2 or 3 minutes. Next put 4 tablespoons flour with the onion and stir until dissolved, then add milk and mix well with other ingredients. Add salt and pepper to season the gravy and stir until gravy has thickened. Serves 6.

Mrs. Ellis Sheppard, Sr.
Columbia

SCALLOPED RHUBARB

3 cups fresh rhubarb (cut
crosswise in ½ inch pieces)
4 Tbs. butter
2 cups soft bread crumbs

1 cup sugar
1 orange rind (grated)
Whipped cream
Orange extract

Wash and wipe the stalks of rhubarb and cut crosswise in ½ inch pieces to make 3 cups. (Do not peel if young and tender.) Melt butter, add bread crumbs, and toss until butter is absorbed. Mix 1 cup sugar with orange rind. Sprinkle bottom of buttered 1 quart pudding dish with 1/3 the crumbs. Cover crumbs with ½ the rhubarb and sprinkle with ½ cup orange-sugar mix. Repeat until crumbs, rhubarb, and orange-sugar are used, leaving layer of crumbs on top. Cover loosely and bake 45 minutes in hot oven. Remove cover and brown quickly. Serve hot with whipped cream sweetened and flavored with orange extract.

Mr. & Mrs. R. D. Coble
Pensacola, Florida

SPINACH RECIPE

2 pkg. frozen spinach
½ pint sour cream
1/3 cup Parmesan cheese
Garlic

Salt
Bread crumbs
Butter

Cook spinach. Drain, squeezing out and discarding all liquid. Add sour cream, Parmesan cheese, garlic, and salt. Put into casserole dish. Sprinkle with bread crumbs, dot with butter. Cook in oven until bubbles.

Mrs. Clement F. Haynsworth, Jr.
Greenville

STUFFED ACORN SQUASH

2 acorn squash
2 Tbs. butter
1 Tbs. brown sugar
¼ tsp. nutmeg

¼ cup light corn syrup
½ cup chopped nuts
½ cup raisins

Cut squash in halves. Bake one hour at 350^0. Remove from oven and scrape out pulp almost to the skin. Add butter, brown sugar and nutmeg to pulp. Beat until smooth. Fold in raisins and nuts. Fill shells with mixture. Place in a shallow baking dish. Drizzle syrup over tops of squash halves. Return to oven set at 400^0 for about 10 minutes.

Mrs. Lucille McMaster
Winnsboro

COUNTRY CLUB SQUASH CASSEROLE

6-8 small squash
2 Tbs. butter
1 Tbs. grated onion
1 bouillon cube
1 egg

½ cup grated sharp cheese
1 cup sour cream
Dash paprika
Salt and pepper to taste

Cut squash into small pieces and cook in small amount of boiling water until perfectly smooth. Add butter, bouillon cube, grated onion, salt and pepper. Add well-beaten egg and blend. Fold in sour cream. Pour into a well-greased, 1-quart baking dish. Make a topping of the crumbs, cheese and paprika. Sprinkle over top of squash. Bake at 350⁰ for 30 minutes.

Mrs. Lucille McMaster
Winnsboro

SCALLOPED SQUASH

2 cups cooked squash
1 egg (well beaten)
1 cup evaporated milk
(or 1 can undiluted
  cheddar cheese soup)

1 cup cracker crumbs
½ stick butter
1 Tbs. sugar
Salt, pepper (to taste)
Grated cheese

Cook squash until tender. Add egg, milk (or soup), sugar, butter, salt, pepper, and cracker crumbs. Mix thoroughly and put in baking dish. Sprinkle grated cheese on top. Cook in slow oven 300⁰ for 45 minutes.

Mrs. Joe Long
Abbeville

STUFFED YELLOW SQUASH

4 small yellow squash
¼ tsp. paprika
¼ tsp. Worcestershire sauce
¼ tsp. curry powder
½ tsp. salt

1 Tbs. butter
1 Tbs. grated onion
¼ cup bread crumbs
Pepper to taste

Steam whole squash until barely tender. Scoop out centers, leaving shell about ½ inch thick. Chop the pulp, add remaining ingredients and blend well. Fill shells with stuffing. Top with ½ cup buttered bread crumbs. Place in a baking dish containing enough water to cover the bottom. Bake at 350⁰ for 10-15 minutes. (Note: Scallop or zucchini may be substituted for yellow squash.)

Mrs. Lucille McMaster
Winnsboro

SQUASH CASSEROLE FOR FREEZER

5 lb. squash
3 eggs (beaten)
1 stick margarine
Salt, pepper to taste

¾ pkg. Pepperidge Farm seasoned
  stuffing
1½ cups cheese (grated)
1 cup onions (chopped)

Boil squash and onions. Salt and pepper to taste. Remove and drain well. Beat margarine and cheese together. Add stuffing, perhaps retaining some for top. Fold in beaten eggs. Pour in greased pan and cool. Wrap in foil and freeze. When ready to use, thaw and bake at 350⁰ for 20 to 25 minutes. Remove foil when almost done.

Mrs. James B. Edwards
Mt. Pleasant

SQUASH CASSEROLE

1½ lbs. yellow squash
1 small jar pimentos
  (chopped)
1 small onion (grated)
1 pkg. Pepperidge Farm
  Cornbread stuffing

1 cup sour cream
1 can cream of chicken
  soup
1 stick melted margarine

Slice, cook, drain, and mash squash. Add other vegetables, soup, and sour cream. Mix stuffing and melted margarine. Line bottom of casserole with part of crumbs, reserving some for top. Pour in squash mixture and sprinkle rest of crumbs. Bake at 350⁰ for 30 minutes. This recipe freezes well.

Mrs. J. L. Brunson
Sumter

215

SQUASH CASSEROLE

1½ lbs. yellow squash, sliced
1½ cups grated cheese
 (sharp cheddar)
1 Tbs. instant minced onion
1 tsp. sugar

Salt to taste
1 can cream of mushroom
 soup
½ box Ritz crackers (broken)

Soak onion in enough water to cover for 5 minutes and drain. Cook squash in small amount of salt water in a saucepan until tender. Add instant onion, sugar, and salt to taste. Heat cream of mushroom soup in a saucepan. Alternate layers of squash mixture, cheese, soup, and crackers until all is used up in casserole. Bake in pre-heated 325⁰ oven for 30 minutes

Mrs. Allen B. Thomas
Aiken

SUMMER SQUASH AND OKRA

This recipe was the lone fortunate result of an unfortunate summer garden. Only the squash and okra survived the unusually hot season, and we had to experiment with recipes for these.

1 onion
1 bell pepper
1 clove of garlic in oil or
 bacon grease
2 small cans of mushrooms
 with liquid

6 to 8 yellow summer squash
20 to 30 pods okra
 (pre-sliced)
Almonds

Sauté onion, pepper, clove of garlic until tender. Add mushrooms and squash, and cook until almost tender (about 10 minutes). Add okra and cook about 5 minutes or until tender. Serve with side dish or sliced almonds.

Mrs. Phriness E. Cox
Chapin

216

WADMALAW SQUASH PIE

8 medium summer squash
1 small onion chopped
¼ cup green pepper (chopped)
1 tsp. Worcestershire sauce
½ tsp. mustard

2 eggs slightly beaten
2 Tbs. evaporated milk
1 cup sharp grated cheese
Dash seasoned salt, pepper,
  and herb seasoning

Cook squash in small amount of water just until tender. Drain. Place in casserole dish and mash well. Sauté onion and pepper in 2 tablespoons of bacon drippings. Add with remaining ingredients to squash and mix well. Top with cracker crumbs and dot with butter. Bake at 350⁰ for 25 to 30 minutes. Serves 6.

Mrs. Adair M. McKoy, III
Wadmalaw Island

YELLOW SQUASH SOUFFLÉ

2½ cups cooked squash
1 tsp. grated onion
1 cup thick white sauce
2 eggs, beaten after separating
  whites and yolks

1 tsp. Worcestershire sauce
Salt and pepper to taste

Puree the cooked squash until smooth. Add grated onion and blend in white sauce. Season well. When somewhat cooled, add egg yolks, then add stiffly beaten egg whites. Pour into a well-buttered baking dish. Bake for 30 minutes in a 350⁰ oven. Serve immediately.

Mrs. Lucille McMaster
Winnsboro

YELLOW SQUASH PUREE

Seed and cut into small pieces 4-6 yellow squash. Steam or cook in small amount of boiling water. Drain well. Mash until smooth with a heavy fork or potato masher. Beat until fluffy. While the squash is still very hot, add a 3-ounce package of cream cheese. Beat until cheese is melted and well blended. Add salt and white pepper to taste.

Mrs. Lucille McMaster
Winnsboro

ZUCCHINI—SPINACH BOATS

3 medium zucchini
1 cup cooked spinach
2 Tbs. butter

2 Tbs. minced onion
2 oz. cream cheese
Buttered bread crumbs

After trimming the ends of the squash, cook whole for 10 minutes. Drain well. Cut in halves lengthwise. Scoop out centers and chop the pulp. Mix with the cooked spinach and onion, which has been sautéed in butter. Place mixture in a saucepan and heat thoroughly. Blend in cream cheese until it melts. Thoroughly dry the squash shells or boats and sprinkle with salt and papper. Fill with hot spinach mixture and top with buttered bread crumbs. Place in a shallow baking dish and bake 15 minutes in an oven preheated to 350^0.

Mrs. Lucille McMaster
Winnsboro

THREE-MINUTE ZUCCHINI FOR SALAD

Wash well several zucchini about three inches long. Plunge them into a saucepan of rapidly boiling water. When water returns to the boil, cook for exactly three minutes. Remove squash from water and immediately put into ice water to stop the cooking process. Pat dry with paper towels. Chill for several hours if possible. Slice crosswise and arrange on salad plates with shredded lettuce. Dress with an oil-and-vinegar dressing or a dressing of your choice.

Mrs. Lucille McMaster
Winnsboro

PLANTATION SWEET POTATOES

2 large cans sweet potatoes
  drained
1 cup orange juice
2 Tbs. butter or margarine
5 Tbs. brown sugar

2 tsp. cinnamon
½ tsp. nutmeg
¼ cup raisins
3 or 4 Tbs. sherry wine
½ tsp. ginger

Place all ingredients in large saucepan. Bring to a boil and then simmer, covered, for 30 minutes. This may be served as is or made into a casserole. Place potatoes in baking dish and mash well to remove all lumps. Add enough juice to make a smooth consistency. Stir in a little more sherry and sugar. Top with pecans or marshmallows and bake at 350⁰ for about 20 minutes. Serves 6.

Mrs. Adair M. McKoy, III
Wadmalaw Island

SWEET POTATO PUDDING

5 cups grated sweet potatoes
5 eggs
2 cups sugar
½ tsp. ground allspice
½ tsp. ground nutmeg

1 tsp. vanilla
2 sticks margarine
1 small can evaporated milk
1 cup water

Combine the above ingredients in a casserole dish and bake at 300⁰ for 3 hours.

Mrs. R. L. Reid
Charlotte, North Carolina

SWEET POTATO SOUFFLÉ

3 cups potatoes
1 cup sugar
½ cup butter

2 eggs
1 tsp. vanilla

Mix and pour in oblong pyrex casserole.

Topping

1 cup coconut
1 cup nuts
1 cup brown sugar

1/3 cup melted butter
1/3 cup flour

Mix all except butter. Pour butter over top. Bake at 300⁰ for 20-30 minutes.

Mrs. J. L. Martin
West Columbia

SWEET POTATO SOUFFLÉ

1 qt. mashed sweet potatoes	½ cup black walnuts (chopped)
½ cup sherry	2 eggs (beaten)
¼ tsp. salt	½ cup butter
½ cup sugar	

Whip all but black walnuts in machine until light. Fold in pan and bake in moderate oven until golden (about 1 hr.). Sprinkle chopped black walnuts on top and serve. Serves 6.

Miss Lola Jaques
Arlington, Virginia

SWEET POTATO SOUFFLÉ WITH BLACK WALNUTS

1 (no. 3) can sweet potatoes	1 tsp. allspice
1 cup white sugar	1 cup black walnuts
4 eggs	Marshmallows
1 tsp. cinnamon	Red cherries
1 tsp. nutmeg	

Dice sweet potatoes, and keep resulting liquid. Blend potatoes and liquid with sugar, eggs and spices. Add nuts. Bake in large casserole for 45 to 60 minutes. When ready to serve, cover top of casserole with marshmallows, red cherries, and nuts.

Mrs. P. B. Hultzendorff
Clemson

CURRIED TOMATOES

6 ripe tomatoes	4 Tbs. sharp cheese
1 cup tomato sauce	(grated)
2 tsp. curry powder	3 Tbs. fresh bread crumbs
2 Tbs. currant jelly	6 bacon slices (crisp)

Preheat oven to 425⁰. Butter shallow baking dish. Peel tomatoes. Remove stem ends. Place tomatoes in baking dish. Combine tomato, sauce, currant jelly, and curry powder. Heat 5 minutes, pour over tomatoes. Sprinkle with bread crumbs and cheese. Bake 15 minutes. Garnish with bacon slices and serve hot. Serves 6.

Mrs. Clement F. Haynsworth, Jr.
Greenville

Contributors

Index

228

229

230

231

232

235

236

TO: THE SANDLAPPER STORE, INC.
P.O. Box 841
Lexington, South Carolina 29072

Please send me _____ copies of **The Sandlapper Cookbook** at $5.95* per copy plus 50c per copy (for postage and handling). Order for 5 or more books postpaid. S.C. residents add 4% sales tax !o the cost of the books.

Name _____

Street _____

City _____

State & Zip _____

* price subject to change

TO: THE SANDLAPPER STORE, INC.
P.O. Box 841
Lexington, South Carolina 29072

Please send me _____ copies of **The Sandlapper Cookbook** at $5.95* per copy plus 50c per copy (for postage and handling). Order for 5 or more books postpaid. S.C. residents add 4% sales tax to the cost of the books.

Name _____

Street _____

City _____

State & Zip _____

* price subject to change

TO: THE SANDLAPPER STORE, INC
P.O. Box 841
Lexington, South Carolina 29072

Please send me_____ copies of **The Sandlapper Cookbook** at $5.95* per copy plus 50c per copy (for postage and handling). Orders for 5 or more books postpaid. S.C. residents add 4% sales tax !o the cost of the books.

Name _____

Street _____

City _____

State & Zip _____

* price subject to change